KARNEVAL

KARNEVAL

KARNEVAL
Touya Mikanagi

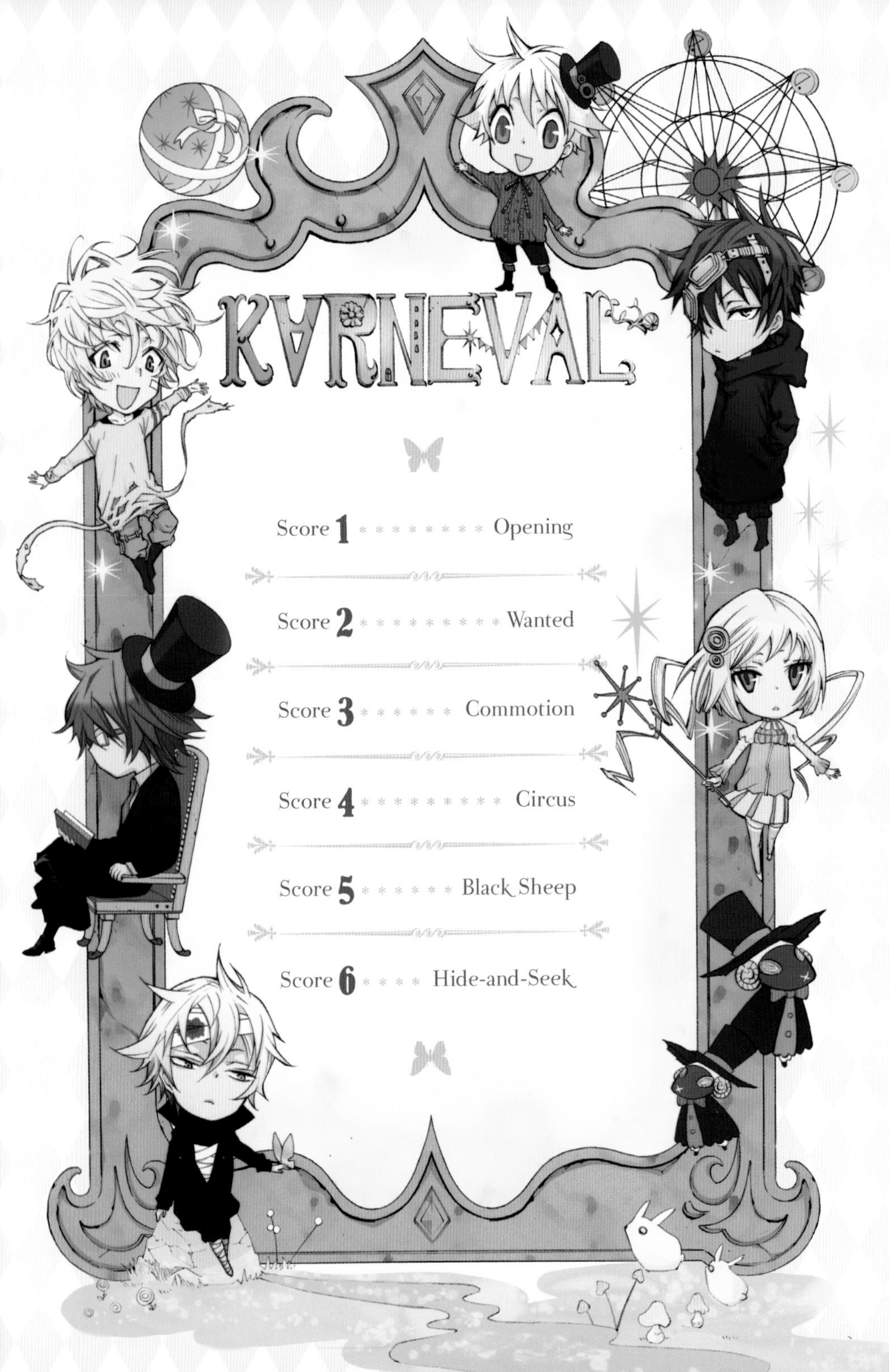

KARNEVAL

KARNEVAL

KARNEVAL

NAI, COME HERE.
IF I WERE TO...
KAROKU.
WHERE HAVE YOU GONE?

Score 1: Opening

DON (BOOM)
DODON (KABOOM)
Karasuna, the Illuminated City
DODON
DON
GUI (YANK)
NGH ...!
JUST HURRY UP AND WALK!!
GA (WHAM)

LADY MINE!!
ONCE AGAIN, YOU'RE LOOKING STILL MORE BEAUTIFUL TODAY!!
WHY, THANK YOU. ♥
WE'VE BROUGHT THE BOY YOU ASKED FOR AS WELL.
NICE WORK ~! ♥
OH MY.
HOW PRECIOUS. ♥
HEY!
TELL THE LADY YOUR NAME!!
GUN (JERK)

... NA—
NAI...
I WANT TO SEE YOU, KAROKU...
I WALKED SO MUCH... WHY AREN'T YOU HERE?
OOOH, HE'S JUST SO INNO-CENT! ♥
I'LL CRUSH YOUR RIVALS FOR YOU BY WAY OF YOUR REWARD!
THANK YOU VERY MUCH.
YOU WOULDN'T MIND IF THEY HAPPENED TO DIE IN THE PROCESS, WOULD YOU?
NIKO (SMILE)
NOT AT ALL. IF THEY WERE TO DIE BY THE HAND OF OUR LADY MINE OF THE NATIONAL SUPREME DEFENSE FORCE "CIRCUS"...
...NO ONE WOULD DOUBT THAT THEY WERE "EVILDOERS."

THERE'S NO NEED TO BE NERVOUS! ♥
YOU AND I ARE GOING TO HAVE LOTS OF FUN TOGETHER NOW!
AREN'T YOU GLAD?
UU... HRRRGH!
URP!
(YOU'RE PRESSING ON MY TUMMY...)
I FEEL SICK...
YOU'RE... HEAVY!
BISHI (SNAP)
JUST WHAT PART OF ME DO YOU FIND SICKENING AND HEAVY!?
DOGO (SLAM)
PIGU (SQUEAL)
SHUUUU (STEAM)
!?

IS THIS ONE OF CIRCUS'S ...!?
WHY?
IS THIS CHILD NOT ONE OF THE USUAL ORPHANS ...?
NO, THEY COULDN'T BE ON TO ME...
AH.
THAT.
IT'S KARO-KU'S...
KAROKU?
WHO WOULD THAT BE?

ALL SET ~!
THE CUTIE PA-TROL'S HEADED OUT!
ALL RIGHT. BACK IT UP.
PI (BEEP) PI
PIII
BOFUN (BLAST)
KARA
KARA (CLATTER)
WHOO-EEEE! ♪
YOU'RE AWE-SOME, MAN!
HOW COME YOU KNOW ABOUT MAKING BOMBS 'N' STUFF?
JUST HURRY UP AND GET IN THERE!
AND LEAVE THE UN-RELATED WOMEN ALONE.

POOON (POP)
GIVE IT BACK!!
UWAAHN!
NO.
WAY!
KURUN (TWIRL)
KURUN
COME ON!
COME AND GET IIIIT! ♥
DA (DASH)
DA
DA
DA
OVER HEEERE!
BAN (WHAM)
GOSHAA (CRASH)
EE!
PARIN (SHATTER)
AH HA HA HA HA HA!
UU...
WHY?
THAT'S DEAR KARO-KU'S—
IT'S NOT "KARO-KU'S."
JIN (STING)
JIN

—EH?
WILL YOU TELL ME ABOUT THIS KAROKU?
HE'S MY FAMILY.
WE LIVED TOGETHER IN THE FOREST.
BUT HE LEFT THAT BRACELET BEHIND AND WENT AWAY SOMEWHERE.
BUMPKINS LIKE YOU BLOW MY MIND!
HOW CAN YOU NOT KNOW WHAT THIS IS!?
IT'S A CIRCUS ID BRACELET!
CIRCUS IS AN ELITE ORGANIZATION THAT FLIES ALL OVER THE CONTINENT, HUNTING DOWN WANTED CRIMINALS!
IT'S NOT SOMETHING THAT A PAIR OF BACKWATER BROTHERS LIKE YOU DESCRIBED WOULD HAVE!
—SO...
...YOUR BROTHER CLEARLY STOLE THIS.

IN WHICH CASE, HIS DISAPPEARANCE MAKES COMPLETE SENSE, YOU KNOW?
I'M SURE HE'S BEEN ARRESTED BY CIRCUS!
STEALING ONE OF THEIR ID BRACELETS MAKES HIM PUBLIC ENEMY NUMBER ONE!

WHAT'S A PUB... LIC... ENEMY ...?
HUH!? YOU MUST BE JOK-ING!?

HOW CAN A HAYSEED LIKE YOU, WHO CAN'T EVEN UNDERSTAND SPOKEN LANGUAGE, EVER HOPE TO FIND SOMEONE IN A CITY LIKE THIS? GIVE IT UP!
KATAN (CLACK)
I'LL KEEP THIS SAFE FOR YOU.

YOU SHOULD JUST STAY HERE.
WITH ME.
BASHI (SMACK)

I CAN'T. I—
I HAVE TO GO TO KAROKU ...!
GUWA (BLAST)
ZUZUN (SHOOM)
BI (BEEP) BI BI
PARA PARA (CRUMBLE)
!?
SU (SWF)
I'LL MAKE YOU FORGET YOUR PAST IN NO TIME.
I HAVE A LITTLE HOUSE-KEEPING TO SEE TO. I'LL BE RIGHT BACK.
AH...

DA (DASH)
BATAN (SLAM)
GACHIN (LOCK)
BAN (BAM)
GATA (RATTLE)
GATA
KAROKU...
PARA
PARA
MISHI (CREAK)
DOGO (CRASH)
BIKUU (JOLT)
GARA (CLATTER)
!?
TO (TMP)
BIN (TWANG)
GOTO (CLUNK)
DO (THUD)
DO

CHIRA (GLANCE)
チラ
BIKU (FLINCH)
ビクッ
DON (THUNK)
どん
...!

GASHAAAN (CRAAASH)
BIKUU
ZAAA (HEAP)
GARA (CLATTER)
GARA
......
RIGHT, THEN.
GUESS I'LL HEAD BACK.
AH! UMM...
ARE YOU GOING OUT-SIDE!?
YEAH... WHY?
I WANT TO LEAVE TOO... BUT...
...I DON'T KNOW HOW TO GET THERE FROM HERE...
ORO (WAVER)
ORO
ZAA (FWOOSH)

SO?
AH!
THAT IS... KARO-KU'S...
WHAT?
IS IT YOURS?
OHH?
...HMM.
I HEARD YOU FROM UP ON THE CEILING.
THAT BRACE-LET OF YOURS ...
IT BELONGS TO A "KAROKU," WAS IT?
IF YOU FILL ME IN ON THE DETAILS AFTER, I'M COOL WITH BREAKING YOU OUTTA HERE.
EH!?
NIKO (SMILE)
THAT SOUNDED PRETTY COOL, HUH?
I'M INTO THAT KINDA THING.

Y—
YES!
PAA (BEAM)
OKAY!
ALL RIGHT!
JAKI (KACHIK)
DEAL!!
GAKIN (KACLANK)
I'M GAREKI.
YOU?
NAI.
OH, THAT RIGHT?
GI (CREAK)

GIGI (CREEEAK)
DON (WHAM)
U- WAH!?
GO (BONK)
GIGII
WHAT THE—!?
BYUU (WHIZ)
DOGA (SMASH)
!!
CAN YOU MOVE !?
WHAT WENT DOWN ?
SHE'S A...
...MON-STER... RUN—
GATA (TREMBLE)
GATA

PAKI (CRACK)
PEKIN (SNAP)
HMM? WANT TO PLAY TAG, DO YOU?
FINE BY ME. LET'S HAVE SOME DEADLY FUN, SHALL WE?
ZU
ZU (ZOOP)
ZU

GA (GRAB)
COME ON!!
GEHO (COUGH)

AND WITH THE SECOND, I SHALL HAVE YOUR INNARDS ...
AND COME THE THIRD STEP, YOU'LL BE A BLOODY BANQUET FOR MY DINNER!
YOU GUYS GO ON!!
BYU (WHIZ)
GUWA (BOOOM)
TCH!
WHY'D YA HAVE TO GO AND FIGHT ME!!?

BAN (WHAM)
WHOA!
BIKU (JUMP)
ZU (SLITHER)
ZU
DOON (BOOM)
BI (BEEP)
BI
BI
HRNN, WHAT NOW?
MAN, THEY SURE ARE PUTTIN' ON A SHOW!
G-GAREKI!?
GAVE ME A SCARE, YA DID...
HA (PANT)
HA
WHAT'S UP? SOMETHING WRONG?
AW, CRAP...
YOU COMIN' THIS WAY WASN'T PART OF THE PLA—
GUSHU (GOOSH)
IT'S BEEN SOME TIME SINCE I'VE DINED.
ZU (LOOM)
WHO SHALL I PUT ON THE MENU FOR TONIGHT?
ZU
ZU
POTA (DRIP)

BOKON (POP)
KUKI (CRICK)
BOKON
GYURU (SHWIRL)
GYU (SHWOOP)
HUH?
LOOK OUT!!
GUWASHI (GRAB)
ZAZAA (SKSHHH)

HUH?
GUSHU (CRUNCH)
PAKI (CRACK)
BUCHI (TEAR)
U-
AAAUGH!?
GUSHU
GA (CHOMP)
GA
—!
GUCHI (CRUNCH)
H-AH!
BAKI (SNAP)
BICHU (SPLATTER)
HEY

...!
GU
(WHIP)
GO
(BUMP)
!?

GWAH...
G-
GAREKI
...!
AGH!!
N-GH...
WHAT ARE YOU DOING!?
HURRY!
HNGH...!
GAH...

JYURU (DRIBBLE)
PAKI (CRACK)
I REALLY DO NEED TO BE BETTER ABOUT EATING.
GW... ...AH!
I'M SO SLOW WHEN I DON'T.
AH!
I OUGHT TO HAVE GOBBLED YOU RIGHT UP INSTEAD OF PLAYING WITH YOU IN BED.
I COULD HAVE CULLED THE LOT OF YOU IN ONE SWOOP IF I HAD.
GAH!..
HELP ME!
GA- GAREKI!? WHAT THE HELL'RE YOU DOING !?
GWAH...
GHRK...
YOU BASTARD! ARE YOU COMPLETELY HEARTLESS!?
AH...

NOW'S OUR CHANCE! C'MON!!
GUN (SPIN)
JYUPA (SLORCH)
ジュパ
EEP ...
GYAAAAH!
...PHEW.

NOW!
I'LL CATCH YOU RIIIIGHT UP, MY DEARS ~!
GYUN (ZHOOOM)
HOW FAAAAR DID YOU GOOOO, HMM ~?
ZAA (VSSSSH)
KACHIRI (KACHINK)
!?
PITA (FREEZE)
KA (FLASH)

DON
(BOOOOM)
GARA
(CLATTER)
GARA
DO
DO
(THUD)
DO
WELCOME BACK,
TSUKUMO-CHAN.

FU (SWOOP)
!
I WAS HAVING TEA ON THE SECOND FLOOR WHILE I WAITED FOR YOU.
I MADE QUICK WORK OF THINGS ON MY END.
HEY ...!
IT'S FINE, IT'S FIIINE~! I MASKED MY PRESENCE BEFORE I JUMPED.
I'M SURE NO ONE SAW THAT JUST NOWWW!
YES, YES.
ANYWAY, NEVER MIND THAT. LET'S HAVE YOUR REPORT ON THE WOMAN.
WE'RE MOVING ON HER RIGHT AWAY.
ZU ZU ZU (FWSH)
PIKU (TWITCH)

GARA (CRUMBLE)

OWWWWWW!
DAMN BRATS!!
SU (SWF)
HM?

OH DEAR ~!

YOU'VE COME ALREADY-YYYYY?

BIKKURIII (SHOCK)

EVERY-THING'S IN SUCH A STATE RIGHT NOW!

HOW EMBAR-RASSING!

I'LL HAVE IT CLEANED UP RIGHT AWAYYY!

IF ONLY YOU'D KEPT COLLECTING MONEY AND DOLLS QUIETLY...
...YOU MIGHT HAVE LIVED...
...JUST A LITTLE LONGER.
GO (GRAB)
BISHA (SPLAT)

THAT WAS NUTS!

HA (PANT)

IS CIRCUS REALLY THAT MESSED UP?
WHAT WAS WITH THAT CRAZY BODY OF HERS?
IS THAT WHAT THE RUMORS MEAN BY CIRCUS'S "SPECIAL POWERS"?
HA

'SWHAT I'D CALL A MONSTER.
HARD TO TELL WHO THE REAL VILLAIN WAS BACK THERE, DON'T YOU THINK?
HA

GUYS WHO EAT HUMANS...
...ARE S'POSED TO BE THE GUARDIANS OF THE LAND?
WHAT A JOKE!
"FROM NOW ON, WE'LL PLAY TOGETHER EVERY DAY, NAI."
HOW MUCH LONGER DO I HAVE TO GO BEFORE I CAN SEE KAROKU AGAIN?
I WANT TO EAT WITH HIM.
MY BODY HURTS ALL OVER.

KAROKU.
GURA (SWAY)
—HUH?

Z8-1
DOSA
(FWUMP)

ARE YOU FOR REAL? UGH, WHAT A PAIN.
"I'M SURE HE'S BEEN ARRESTED BY CIRCUS!"
CIRCUS... WHAT IS CIRCUS? IF I GO THERE, CAN I SEE HIM?
—WHOA, WHOA, HOLD UP...

べシ
BESHI (SMACK)
HEY!?
NAI!!
KAROKU—

SCORE 2: Wanted

HA (PANT)
は…
HE CHILLED OUT AFTER DRINKING SOME WATER, BUT...
...HE STILL REFUSES EAT!?
TCH!
HEY, NAI!
STAY PUT!!
IF YOU GET THIRSTY AGAIN, THERE'S THE WATER!
I'M GONNA GO ROUND UP SOME GRUB, SO JUST STAY HERE 'N' DREAM OR SOMETHING TILL I GET BACK!

HE DIDN'T COME TODAY...

WHY?

はー
HA

A RED PUDDLE...

THIS...

KAROKU...

GUESS THE PROFITS ARE IN LINE WITH THE HAIRY SITUATION...
KUH KUH ...
FENCED THAT STUFF AT THE SWEETEST RATE YET!!

HERE, POPS.
HEYY, GAREKI! LONG TIME NO SEE!
WE HAVE SOME GREAT RAGGIS TODAY!
OKAY, I'LL TAKE IT.
AND WHAT'S THE MOST NUTRITIOUS MEAT YOU'VE GOT RIGHT NOW?

WHAT'S THIS!? DIDJA GO AND GET A GIRL KNOCKED UP!?
HOW MANY TIMES DID YA DO THE DEED?
STOP TALKING CRAP.
YOU'RE THE PICTURE OF A DIRTY OLD MAN...
MEAT!

WHOA, NOW!
LIIIIKE WE TOLD YA, KID! CIRCUS JUST POPS OUTTA THIN AIR! COULD BE ANYWHERE!
NOW THAT YOU GOT YOUR ANSWER, YOU GOTTA GIVE US SOMETHIN' BY WAY OF A THANK-YOU!
LOOKS LIKE THIS IS THE ONLY THING OF VALUE HE'S GOT?
NO!

GIVE IT BACK!!

GA (SNATCH)

HEY!?

CRAP ...!

A PEACE-KEEPER ...!

HOLD IT!!

WHAT DO YOU THINK YOU'RE DOING !!?

ARE YOU ALL RIGHT, SON?
—HUH? ISN'T THIS BRACELET ...!?
HUH!?
SO THEN...
YOU ...!?

SIGN: PEACEKEEPER HQ
ARE YOU A TOTAL MORON!?
OF COURSE, I'M EMBARRASSED FOR ASSUMING A BOY LIKE THAT WAS A MEMBER OF CIRCUS BASED JUST ON HIS POSSESSION OF THAT BRACELET...
WHAT KIND OF CIRCUS MEMBER WOULDN'T BE ABLE TO TAKE CARE OF HIS OWN BRACE-LET!?
THIS IS OBVIOUSLY A FAKE CREATED FOR SOME NEFARIOUS PURPOSE!!
ABSURD!
... TAKE A LOOK AT THIS.
I HAD THE BRACELET ANALYZED, JUST IN CASE.
HAD I NOT SEEN THESE RESULTS, I WOULD'VE COME TO THE SAME CONCLUSION AS YOU, CHIEF...
WHAT... KIND OF VALUES ARE THESE ...!?
NO... IMPOSSIBLE. THERE'S NO WAY SOME COUNTER-FEITER COULD'VE GOTTEN THEIR HANDS ON MATERIALS OF THIS CALIBER...
THIS COULD ONLY HAVE BEEN CREATED USING A RELATED METHOD OF ASSEMBLY TO THE REAL THING.
BUT AS I THINK IT'S OBVIOUS THAT THE BOY COULDN'T BE CIRCUS, I THOUGHT I MIGHT DO A LITTLE INVESTIGATING AND PUT TOGETHER A REPORT HERE ON...
—? CHIEF JING?

HAVE YOU INFORMED ANYONE OTHER THAN ME ABOUT THIS?
NO, NOT YET.
I THOUGHT I SHOULD REPORT MY FINDINGS TO YOU FIRST, CHIEF—
...IS THAT RIGHT?
WHEN I SAID I WANTED TO GO TO CIRCUS, I WAS BROUGHT HERE...
IS THIS CIRCUS ...?
WILL I BE ABLE TO SEE KAROKU...?
DOKI (BADUM)
DOKI
SHU (ZWIP)
DOKIN (BADUM)
KAROKU ...!
PAN (BLAM)

HUH ...? THE MAN FROM BEFORE ...?
A RED... PUDDLE?
DOSA (WHUMP)
HOLD THIS.
!?
GYU (PRESS)
ぎゅっ
HAA (PANT)
はあ
YOU...
... WERE THE ONE WHO SHOT THIS MAN.

THAT BRACELET'S TOO GOOD FOR A RAGGEDY LITTLE BRAT LIKE YOU.
I'LL PUT IT TO MUCH BETTER USE.
SCARY...
IF I SELL IT ON THE BLACK MARKET, I'LL BE ABLE TO PAY BACK THAT LOAN.
MY LUCK'S FINALLY TURNING AROUND.
AND NOW, WITH YOUR PRINTS ALL OVER MY SUBORDINATE'S GUN, I'LL TAKE IT BACK FROM YOU AND AVENGE HIS DEATH!
THIS PERSON...
GATAN (CLANK)
...MAKES ME FEEL SICK...!!

HE MADE A RUN FOR IT... WELL, THAT'S FINE.
PI (BEEP)
IT'S ME.
THE SUSPECT WE WERE INTERROGATING HAS SHOT AN OFFICER DEAD AND IS ON THE RUN. HE'S ARMED AND DANGEROUS.
IF I USE MY MEN, I'LL HAVE A BRAT LIKE HIM BACK IN CUSTODY IN NO TIME.
BARA (SCATTER)
BARA
DUE TO THE CULPRIT'S VIOLENT NATURE, THE USE OF FIREARMS IS PERMITTED ON SIGHT!
?
AVENGE OUR FALLEN BROTHER!
FIRE!!

GONE
THAT LITTLE ...!
BRAT!
HE'S SO DEAD.
GAN (CLANG)

WE'VE BEEN BEATEN TO THE PUNCH.
AWW...
DEAR ME...
THEY CERTAINLY WORKED FAST.

PIRORIRON (RINGALING)
WHAT A SHAME.
AT THE VERY LEAST, THIS PROVES THAT THIS MINE WOMAN WAS INDEED INVOLVED...
...
YES?
...WHAT?
ALL RIGHT...
UNDER-STOOD.
HAA (PANT)
HA
HAA
KAROKU MIGHT REALLY HAVE BEEN IN THAT PLACE...
IF I GO BACK, I WONDER IF THAT SCARY PERSON WILL BE THERE TOO... BUT MAYBE JUST ONCE MORE—

GA (GRAB)
DAN (WHAM)
HEYYY, YOU.
DID I OR DIDN'T I TELL YOU TO STAY PUT, HUHHH?
GIRI (GRIND)
GIRI
PASUN (POOMF)
PASUN
JITA
JITA (FLAIL)
SO YOU'D RUN OFF WITHOUT A WORD AFTER SOMEONE SAVES YOUR BUTT, HUH!?
GIRI
GIRI
I EVEN WENT OUT TO BUY YOU FOOD, Y'KNOW?
HAVING NO MANNERS IS A REAL CRIME, DON'TCHA THINK?

YOU!
LOST THE BRACE-LET!?
BIKUU (JUMP)
……
I…
…WANTED TO LOOK FOR KAROKU.
I WANTED TO SEE HIM…
SO I THOUGHT I'D TRY TO GO TO THAT CIRCUS PLACE…
I…
…WANT TO SEE HIM…
I'M SORRY, GAREKI…
—
FOR YOUR INFORMATION…

...YOU'RE TOTALLY THE TYPE TO DIE YOUNG.
きょとん
KYOTON (BLANK)
YOU KEEP GETTING CAPTURED AND SET UP LEFT AND RIGHT!
EVEN IF YOU DID NOTHING, THERE'RE STILL PLENTY OF PEOPLE WHO'D TRY TO WALK ALL OVER YOU TO SATISFY THEIR OWN GREED!
STOP TRUSTING PEOPLE LIKE AN IDIOT ALL THE TIME.
AT LEAST GET YOUR HANDS DIRTY ENOUGH TO PROTECT YOURSELF!
イラ…
IRA (IRK)
WHY AM I SAYING ALL THIS TO HIM?
I WAS PLANNING TO USE HIM AND LOSE HIM TOO.

YEP! I UNDERSTAND.
?
I'LL BECOME DIRTY LIKE YOU, GAREKI! OKAY!?
BFF!
I MEANT GROW A BRAIN, YOU MORON!
GIRI (GRIND)
GIRI
?
?

NOW GET OUTTA THOSE WANTED POSTER DUDS!!

BASA (RUSTLE)

OOF!

WE'RE GETTING IT BACK.

?

NIYA (GRIND)

YOUR TREASURE.

HYOKO (POP)

CHIEF!
FIVE MINUTES AFTER I GET INSIDE...
IS THAT THE GUY?
GAREKI
NAI
...PRESS THAT BUTTON, AND THEN HIDE WHERE I JUST SHOWED YOU.
DON'T SCREW UP.
'K-'KAY.
DOKI (BADUM)
DOKI
JIIII (STARE)
FIVE MINUTES...
FIVE MINUTES?
...WAIT, HOW LONG IS THAT?
GOODNESS! COLOR ME IMPRESSED! A YOUNG MAN LIKE YOURSELF...
...COMING OUT HERE TO EXPRESS YOUR THANKS TO US FOR HELPING YOU OUT.
WE WERE JUST DOING OUR JOB, AFTER ALL!
KA (CLICK)
KA

WHAT A PRO-ACTIVE KID!
HA HA...
AND ON TOP OF THAT, YOU EVEN WANTED A TOUR OF HQ TO GET CLOSER TO YOUR DREAM OF JOINING THE FORCE SOMEDAY...
HA...
HRMFF ...!
WHAT IS THAT TWERP DOING?
IT'S BEEN TWENTY MINUTES...
THE TOUR'S FREAKIN' OVER!!
ドン
DON (BOOM)
モク モク...
MOKU MOKU (BILLOW)
WHA—!?
AN EXPLOSION!?
YEEEP!
YOU'RE LATE, DAMMIIIIIIT—!!
I'M SORRY, SON. YOU'LL HAVE TO SEE YOURSELF OUT!!
WELL, FRANKLY, THANKS TO THE DELAY... I'VE GOT THE ENTIRE LAYOUT OF THE STATION IN MY HEAD NOW...
HAH ...!
HAAH!

HFF!
精肉所
HFF...
WALL: MEAT-PACKING AREA
WHAT IS THIS!?
MOKU (BILLOW)
MOKU
WHY, IT'S NOTHING BUT SMOKE AND A LOUD BANG?
WAS IT JUST A PRANK!?
JIJI (BZZT)
I DON'T SENSE ANYONE IN HERE.
BACHI (ZAP)
SHU (SHWIP)
WHAT A POINTLESSLY HUGE OFFICE.
AFTER THAT EXPLOSION, I OUGHTA HAVE THIS PLACE TO MYSELF FOR A LITTLE WHILE...
PI (BEEP) PI
......
SHUN (SHOOSH)
WHY THE HELL DO I HAVE TO PUT MY ASS ON THE LINE AND GO TO THE BOMB SITE!?
TOO SOOOON!!
DON'T YOU HAVE WORK TO DO!?

GATA (CLATTER)
ガタ
HMPH!
PAKA (POP)
パカッ
UIN (VWEE)
ヴィン
KACHA (CLICK)
カチャ
KACHA
カチャ
THAT'S ...
...
HEY.
GON (BONK)
ゴンッ
WE'RE LEAVING, DIMWIT.
GUSHA (RUFFLE)
ぐしゃ
SO, ABOUT THAT KAROKU GUY...

WAS KAROKU THERE!?
HELL NO!
LIKE I'D KNOW HIM ANYWAY.
ANYWAY, THAT WAS PEACE-KEEPER HQ, NOT CIRCUS!
I THINK YOU'VE GOT THE WRONG IDEA ABOUT "CIRCUS." IT'S NOT A PLACE. IT'S THE NAME OF A GOVERNMENT AGENCY!
WHAT'S WITH YOU?
I DON'T UNDERSTAND.
AND IT LOOKS LIKE THAT BRACELET YOU HAD IS THEIR "ID."
MEANING IT'S A GOOD BET YOUR "KAROKU" IS ONE OF THEM.
ACTUALLY, WITH THE CHAOS BACK AT THE MANSION, I DIDN'T QUITE CATCH IT, SO REMIND ME AGAIN WHY YOU'RE ALL HELL-BENT ON FINDING THIS "KAROKU" GUY?
I HEARD THAT MINE CHICK SAY YOU WERE BROTHERS OR SOMETHING.
KAROKU WAS ALWAYS WITH ME.
WHERE ARE YOUR PARENTS?
PAR-ENTS?

WELL, IT'S NOT THAT WEIRD FOR A KID NOT TO KNOW HIS PARENTS, BUT... HMM?

KAROKU WASN'T COMING, SO I GOT LONELY AND WENT TO GO GET HIM...

...AND I FOUND THIS BIG, RED PUDDLE, AND THEN LOTS OF LITTLE ONES ALL THE WAY TO THE OCEAN...

...AND I FOUND THE BRACELET THERE ON THE GROUND.

RED PUDDLES?

WAIT, ARE WE TALKING ABOUT PUDDLES OF "BLOOD" HERE?

YOU REALLY DON'T KNOW WHAT BLOOD IS!?

THEN HE MUST'VE BEEN MIXED UP IN SOME SERIOUS TROUBLE.

SOUNDS TO ME LIKE SOMEONE ABDUCTED HIM, DON'T YOU THINK?

EITHER THAT, OR THEY DRAGGED HIM TO THE WATER AND TOSSED HIM IN...

WAIT, HOLD UP. WOULDN'T THAT MEAN HE'S DEAD?

THE MORE I HEAR, THE LESS THIS "KAROKU" SOUNDS LIKE CIRCUS...

IS THIS NAI KID GONNA BECOME SOMEONE IMPOR-TANT TO ME?

OR DO I CUT HIM LOOSE HERE?

THAT PISSES ME OFF.
I DON'T WANNA SEE A GUY LIKE HIM PROFIT.
?
BUT IF I DITCH HIM NOW, THAT SHADY CHIEF'S PLAN'LL PAN OUT, HUH?
WHETHER OR NOT THAT ID BRACELET IS THE REAL DEAL...
...AND THE MATTER OF KAROKU'S EXISTENCE TOO...
GUESS THERE'S NO TELLING NAI'S VALUE UNTIL I CAN CONFIRM THIS STUFF WITH CIRCUS.
NAI, LISTEN UP, OKAY?
YOU'RE THE ONLY WITNESS TO THAT GUY'S CRIME.
NO MATTER WHAT YOU SAY, ODDS ARE HE'LL MAKE SURE YOU WIND UP DEAD.
YOUR TESTIMONY'LL NEVER MAKE IT TO THE TOP GUYS.
SO FORGET REACHING OUT TO THE PEACEKEEPERS.
YOUR ONLY CHOICE IS TO GO OVER THEIR HEADS AND STRAIGHT TO CIRCUS.

TO DO THAT, YOU'LL PROBABLY HAVE TO GO TO A BIGGER CITY AND GET OUT AND ABOUT.
THAT CHIEF'S PLANNING ON SELLING OFF THE BRACELET TOMORROW.
THAT'S WHEN WE'LL GET IT BACK!
THEN, WE'LL HAVE TO GET OUTTA THIS TOWN IN A FLASH.
WHAT ABOUT YOU, GAREKI?
HUH?
I'LL BE LONELY WITHOUT YOU.
YOU'RE NICE, GAREKI.

SFX: PUTSU (PRICKLE) PUTSU

IF I'M GOING, I GOTTA GET SOME KINDA **BENEFIT** OUT OF IT, SEE?
BENE-FIT?
MIS-TER NICE GUY...

IN SHORT, YOU NEED TO GIVE ME SOME-THING.

...IS KAROKU'S...

YOUR BRACELET WOULD DO NICELY.

BUT ... ... THAT'S ...

WHEN WE GET IT BACK, YOU CAN GIVE IT TO ME.

THAT WAS THE PLAN FROM THE START, AFTER ALL.

AFTER WE MAKE SURE KAROKU'S OKAY WITH IT FIRST.

HE MIGHT BE DEAD FOR ALL WE KNOW.

AND IF HE'S ALIVE AND NEEDS IT BACK, I'LL STILL PROBABLY GET SOME REWARD FOR TAKING CARE OF THIS KID.

O...
OKAY!
THE EXCHANGE
WAREHOUSE #51, 1:30 A.M.
TODAY'S THE DAY I SAY GOOD-BYE TO A LIFE OF MAKING ENDS MEET!
KA
KA (CLICK)
AND ONCE THE CASH COMES IN, I CAN SAY GOOD-BYE TO MY OLD LADY TOO...
KA
KA
HA (GASP)
YOU ...!

WAIT!!
I NEED TO CALL FOR BACKUP... NO, I CAN'T!
IF THE PEACEKEEPERS SHOW UP HERE, MY BUYER MIGHT WIND UP THINKING I WENT AND SNITCHED. IT COULD BLOW THE WHOLE DEAL!
I'LL KILL HIM MYSELF.
HFF!
HFFF!
I'M SCARED.
IT'S HIM.
GAREKI!

DON (WHAM)
ZUZAA (SKSSH)
!?
ZARI (CRUNCH)
YOU JING OF THE PEACE-KEEPERS?
WHAT ARE YOU DOING IN A PLACE LIKE THIS?
THE BOSS IS ALREADY HERE, YA KNOW?
AH ...
YOU TRYIN' TO BACK OUT NOW?
TCH ...!
PSYCH!
WHAT ...!?
NO, OF COURSE NOT! JUST ONE MOMENT, PLEASE. I'LL GO TO HIM RIGHT NOW!
JIRI (SKFF)
GOOD LUCK.

HEY, YOU CAN COME OUT NOW.
ビクゥッ
DOKUU (QUIVER)
NN?
WHAT?
ガタガタ
GATA (TREMBLE)
GATA
ブルブル
BURU (SHAKE)
BURU
ARE YOU COLD?
SO PATHETIC!
THAT WAS SCARY...
HERE WE GO!
ゴソッ
GOSO (DIG)
AH!

THANK YOU!!
THAT CHIEF GUY'S BEEN RUNNING FOR AROUND FIVE MINUTES.
PI (BEEP)
PO (BOOP)
PA (BAP)
PI
HE SHOULD BE ARRIVING AT HIS DESTINATION RIGHT ABOUT NOW.
HEH ...!
GAREKI?
WHAT ARE YOU DOING?
HMM?
PAKA (POP)
I'M KINDLY PLAYING A REQUIEM FOR OUR PAL.
PIII
ALARM ACTIVATION SWITCH
Siren Alarm: ON
Set to activate in 1 minute.
Back

チカッ
CHIKA (FLASH)
WAIT —!
PLEASE, JUST WAIT A SECOND!
THIS CAN'T BE...!
IT WAS RIGHT HERE ...!
I'M NOT INTERESTED IN WHAT WAS OR COULD NOT HAVE BEEN.
YOU NEVER EVEN HAD IT IN THE FIRST PLACE, DID YOU?
NO...
THIS IS...!

A SIREN... AH, I SEE.
SO THIS WAS ALL A PLOY BY THE PEACE-KEEPERS TO LURE US OUT, HM?
UUUU
BIIII
BIII (WEEE)
!?
NO—
THOUGHT YOU COULD SET US UP, DID YOU?
I DON'T KNOW WHAT—
PAN (BLAM)
UUU (OOOO)
NAI!
WHAT ARE YOU DOING!? THIS WAY!!

PUSHUUU
(PSSSHT)
E31

KUWA (ROAR)
IF WE MISS THIS TRAIN 'COS OF YOUR DILLY-DALLYING, WE'LL HAVE TO WAIT HALF A DAY BEFORE THERE'S ANOTHER ONE!!
SHAAA (HISSS)
I'M SORRY!
WANTED FUGITIVE.
DISGUISE
GAGON (KACLUNK)
EH?
ZAWA (BUZZ)
GAGON
PUSHUUU
WAH!?
IT'S LEAVING!!
ZEE (WHEEZE)
ZEE
SHUU (SHWOO)
GET IN FROM THE WINDOW!!
GAGON

SHUU (WHOOSH)
SHUU
MAMA, HOW COME THE CONDUCTOR'S DOOR DIDN'T OPEN?
THEY'VE ALREADY LEFT THE STATION?
SOMETHING MUST HAVE HAPPENED ...
BATA (SCRAMBLE)
BATA
PI (BEEP)

A DISTRESS CALL FROM TRAIN E31!
UNKNOWN PERSONS HAVE INFILTRATED THE TRAIN'S CAB!!
THEY'VE BEEN HIJACKED!!

I WONDER IF I'LL GET TO SEE HIM.

KAROKU—

Score 3: Commotion

WHERE-ABOUTS IS THE E31 AT PRESENT!?
HAVE ALL THE STATIONS BEEN ALERTED!?
YES, SIR!!
GA (WHOOM)
GA
GA
GA
TATAN (KACLACK)
KIIIN (RIIING)
IIN
?
?

HM? ?
HM?
......
WHAT ARE YOU DOING?
IT'S ANNOYING.
I HEAR AN...
...ODD SOUND.
SOUND?
TATATAN
TATAN
SOUNDS PRETTY NORMAL TO ME. QUIET, EVEN...
WAIT, BESIDES US, THERE'S NO ONE ELSE HERE...
?
?
...IS THERE?

TO (TMP)
GAREKI? WHERE ARE YOU GOING?
SOMETHING FEELS OFF. I'M GONNA TAKE A QUICK LOOK.
YOU'LL JUST GET IN MY WAY, SO GO BACK TO YOUR—
MEKI (CRACK)
GAN (WHAM)

?
... HUH?
HYUN (WHIP)
ZOKU (CHILL)
WHAT THE HELL? THE TRAIN'S ON THE MOVE, BUT HE DROPPED DOWN THROUGH THE R—
CHA (SCHIK)
ZUGA (THWAK)

GUH...!?

DOSA (WHUMP)

GO (BONK)

KURU (TURN)

USING CHILDREN AS LOOK-OUTS...

!?

GATA (SHAKE)

GATA

THE PERSON WHO CAME DOWN FROM THE SKY...

...WENT "THWAK!" TO GAREKI...

TRAIN TICKET.

SCARY...

OH?

HE HAS A TICKET...

ER...

GEHO (COUGH)

UGH...

OW...

OHH!

INNOCENT BYSTANDERS...

IT CAME FROM THE BACK!

BATA (STOMP)

BATA

BATA

THOSE LOUD BANGS!

GARA (SHHNK)

BA (WHAP)
WHO'RE YOU!? ARE YOU HERE TO TAKE BACK THE CEO!?
IF YOU BOYS AREN'T WITH THEM, YOU SHOULD HAVE SAID AS MUCH.
STAND BACK, STAND BACK.
HUNH ...?
SUUU (SWFFF)
ZUKI ZUKI (THROB)
OR ELSE YOU'LL BE MISTAKEN FOR ONE OF THEIR LOT, YOU KNOW?
ZUBA (ZSHHK)
DOSA (WHUMP)
DOSA
KYAAAH!
ZURU
ZURU (DRAG)
WHAT IS HIS DEAL !?
AN-NOY-ING JERK ...
DOKI DOKI (BADUM)
~~~
~~~

HYOKO (POP)
...GAREKI.
THERE ARE LOTS OF PEOPL—
GO (BONK)
I TOLD YOU TO CUT THAT OUT!
AND!
DON'T GO PEEKING IN THE WINDOW SO CARELESSLY!
DO YOU WANT THEM TO FIND YOU!?
YOU IDIOT!!
SHAAA (HISSS)
BUKU (FOAM)
ぶくぶく
BUKU
IN ORDER FOR THE COMPANY TO SURVIVE, LAYOFFS WERE UNAVOIDABLE.
AND YOU CALL MY ACTIONS DIRTY, BUT...
...HERE YOU ARE, DRAGGING MY INNOCENT GRAND-DAUGHTER INTO THIS MESS FOR YOUR OWN AIMS.
GATA (SHAKE)
ガタガタ
GATA
ARE WE NOT THE SAME?

SH—
SHUT UP! SHUT UP!!
AHH ...
SO THEY GOT DOWNSIZED, AND NOW THEY'RE OUT FOR BLOOD?
NOT THAT I GIVE A DAMN.
DOESN'T LOOK LIKE IT'LL GET WORKED OUT ANYTIME SOON—

GAREKI.
THAT GIRL IS SHAKING.
TRYING TO STAY HIDDEN THIS TIME...
I THINK SHE'S JUST SCARED?
I'LL BET SHE WANTS TO GET OUTTA HERE QUICK.
MAKES TWO OF US!
WE'RE GOING TOO FAST TO JUMP OFF.
SAFEST OPTION'S PROBABLY HIDING UNTIL THE TRAIN STOPS...

I WAS REALLY HAPPY WHEN GAREKI TOOK ME AWAY FROM THAT PLACE...

CAN I DO THAT TOO...?

......

NAI.

C'MON, WE'RE GOING BACK TO—

GARA (SLIDE)

HUH!?

WHO ARE YOU!?
WHAT ARE YOU DOING HERE...!?
KYUIN (PING)
GA (GRAB)
PAN (BLAM)
PAN
THOSE TWO...
GO GET 'EM!!
HA (GASP)
ZEE (WHEEZE)
YOU—!
SHURU (WHIRL)

I JUST DON'T GET YOU AT ALL!!
GRAAR!
ズボ ZUBO (ZHVOOM)
ボ BO
ボ BO
?
?
ゴトッ GOTO (THUNK)
ゴト GOTO
TSUKUMO.
GO AFTER THOSE BOYS, PLEASE.
ROGER!
YOU'VE HAD ENOUGH, I TRUST. SO PUT AN END TO THIS NOW.
DESTRUCTION TO TEMPER DISCONTENT IS MERELY EMPTY FOLLY.

I ...!
......!
NO —!
HE KICKED US TO THE CURB LIKE TRASH!!
NO!!
YOU CAN'T EVEN IMAGINE HOW MUCH WE'VE SUF-FERED ...!
JARA (JANGLE)
HA (GASP)
WAIT!!
WHAT IS THIS!?
BUCHI (SNAP)

IT'S THE SWITCH TO DETONATE THE BOMBS WE PLANTED IN EACH OF THE TRAIN CARS. THEY'RE SET TO GO OFF IN ORDER FROM THE REAR!
THERE'S NO DEVICE TO HALT THE SEQUENCE.
AND IF THE TRAIN STOPS, ALL THE BOMBS ARE SET TO EXPLODE SIMULTA-NEOUSLY.
I'VE ALREADY HIT THE SWITCH.
THE CEO WILL DIE! AND I'M SORRY, BUT SO WILL ALL OF YOU...!
HERE THEY COME.
HIDE!
BA (LEAP)

HOW MANY ARE THERE ...!?
!?
THE WOMAN THEY WERE HOLDING CAPTIVE TOO!?
WHY ...?
HA (GASP)
LEAVE HER ALONE!!
SHE'S AN UNARMED WOMAN ...!
GA (GRAB)
GO (WHAM)
WAH!
AH?

ZUDAN (KAWHAM)
YOU'RE JUST REGULAR PASSENGERS, AREN'T YOU? I'LL PROTECT YOU.
SHE TOSSED THEM...
SUCHA (STEP)
HUH?
KIIIII (SKREEE)
THAT SOUND ...
UWAHN!
!?
DON (BOOM)
GUI (GRIP)

GOOOOOOO (FWOOOOH)
!!?
AN EXPLOSION ...!?
... HEY!
ARE YOU OKAY!?
YEAH.
I HEARD AN ODD SOUND...
...ODD SOUND?
WAIT A SECOND, DIDN'T HE...
...PULL US DOWN BEFORE THE EXPLOSION!?
THEN THEY DIDN'T JUST HIJACK THE TRAIN...
...THEY PLANTED BOMBS IN IT TOO!?
... COME ON...!
GYO (GAPE)
GUI (GRAB)
ARE ALL OF YOU ALL RIGHT!?
RUN TO THE FRONT OF THE TRAIN, NOW!!

WHAT ARE YOU STOPPING FOR!?
COME ON!!
BUT, GAREKI...
THE NOISE GOT LOUDER AT THE SAME SPOT IN THE LAST CAR...
IIII (REEE)
FORGET THAT!
!?
PITA (FREEZE)
GARA (RATTLE)
...
HAA (HFF)
I'M GETTING HOT...
HEY, YOU...
WE JUST GOT ON THIS TRAIN SO WE COULD GET TO THE NEXT TOWN.
CAN YOU TELL US WHAT THE HECK IS GOING ON HERE?
HM?
ZEE (PANT)
HAA
ZEE

...
...
...SO, IN SHORT...
...WITH MANY APOLOGIES, YOU BOYS WILL SOON BE...
!!
WHAT HAPPENED!?
H-HE...
HE SWALLOWED SOMETHING AND...
I'LL MAKE HIM VOMIT IT BACK UP!
HE MADE SURE HE COULDN'T TELL US WHERE HE'D HIDDEN THEM...
THIS IS BAD.
ZUZUN (GAGONG)
!?
THAT JOLT JUST NOW...
ACCORDING TO FOUR-EYES, THE KIDNAPPERS HID BOMBS IN ALL THE TRAIN CARS...
THAT MUST'VE BEEN THE NEXT CAR BLOWING UP TOO...
...AND NOW THAT THEY'VE ACTIVATED THEM, THEY'LL BLOW IN ORDER FROM THE LAST CAR TO THE FIRST...
I'D PROBABLY BE ABLE TO DEFUSE THEM...
...BUT SINCE WE DON'T KNOW WHERE THEY'RE HIDDEN, WE WOULDN'T FIND THEM IN TIME...
AWA (PANIC) AWA
TE (TROT) TE TE

SUTON (SIT)
すとん
DOKI (BABMP) DOKI ドキドキ
NAI... WAIT A SECOND ...
I CAN'T GET A SIGNAL HERE...THERE MUST BE SOME KIND OF INTER-FERENCE IN THE AIR.
PAN (KLACK)
WHAT WAS HE SAYING ABOUT A SOUND...?
TSU-KUMO.
FIRST OF ALL, WE...
!
...INTER-FERENCE!?
THE SOUND'S REALLY LOUD.
GAREKI.
IT CAN'T BE...
BUT STILL ...
THE NOISE GOT LOUDER AT THE SAME SPOT IN THE LAST CAR.

...WHAT'VE WE GOT TO LOSE IF WE'RE DYING ANYWAY?
NAI!
FOUR-EYED JERK-WAD!
LISTEN UP!!
FOUR-EYED JERK-WAD
UH...
...
GYO (SHOCK)
WE MAY JUST HAVE A CHANCE!
COME ON!!
......
NAI! WHERE DOES THAT SOUND GET LOUDEST!?

ALL RIGHT, THEN.
EH?
UMM...
AT THE JUNCTION ...
!
STEP BACK.
ジャキ
JAKIN (SCHING)
ガン
GAN (GRAANK)
HERE...
AH...!

CHIKA (FLASH)
CHIKA
IT'S REALLY HERE!
SERIOUSLY?
BA (HALT)

BUT THE MAIN BODY ISN'T A BOMB...IT'S A SIGNAL DEVICE!
THE BASE IS MADE BY S.T. COMPANY, MODEL NUMBER 293. IT'S BEING USED AS A RADIO-WAVE CONTROLLER!?

I CAN'T GUESS WRONG HERE. LOOK CLOSELY AT THE ARRANGEMENT OF THE PARTS, GAREKI!
WHAT WAS IT DESIGNED TO DO!?

THIS PATH...
...I THINK IT FUNCTIONS TO TRANSMIT AN ARMING SIGNAL TO THE BOMB IN THE NEXT CAR, JUST BEFORE THIS ONE EXPLODES.

......
AND THIS...
THIS IS A VIBRATION SENSOR THAT ALLOWS THE BOMB TO DETECT WHETHER THE TRAIN IS STILL IN MOTION.
IT LOOKS LIKE THESE WON'T EXPLODE WITHOUT THE SIGNAL FROM THE PREVIOUS CAR'S BOMB.

MEANING WHAT?
I DON'T KNOW HOW BIG A SIGNAL RANGE THESE THINGS HAVE, BUT...
...IF WE SEVERED THE REAR CARS BEFORE THE ARMING SIGNAL REACHES THE FRONT CARS, WE SHOULD BE SAFE!!

THAT'S A USEFUL ANSWER.
YOU TWO, STEP BACK!
BOU (GLOW)
I'M GOING TO SEVER THE REAR CARS.
WHAT'S THAT LIGHT?
HIS CANE?
BUT IT'S DIFFERENT FROM BEFORE.
WHERE IS IT COMING FROM?
SUU (SWFF)
VAKUUM.

KA
(FLASH)
GA
(WHOOM)
GA
GA
GA
DOON
(BOOM)
GAAA
(HOOONK)
TATAN
(KACLUNK)
TATAN
MISHIRI
(SKRREESH)

DON
DON
DON
GOOOOO (HOOONK)
ゴオォォォ…
HA (GASP)
はっ
…!
THE SIGNAL…! IT'S STOPPED!
SHIN (SILENT)
シン…
LOOKS LIKE WE'RE IN THE CLEAR.
THANK YOU.
…!
HAA (HFFF)
はぁ
SOME-HOW…
…I'M TOTALLY EXHAUSTED NOW.
BESHI (WHAP)
べしっ
?
AH!
WE LEFT OUR LUGGAGE AT OUR SEATS!
THEY'VE BEEN BLOWN TO SMITHEREENS…
TATAN
TATAN

GAREKI? WHERE ARE WE GOING NOW?
WHERE DO YOU THINK!?
KEEP YOUR FACE HIDDEN!!
ANYWAY, THE PEACE-KEEPERS ARE ARRIVING.
DON'T FORGET THAT YOU'RE WANTED BY THEM!
GI (GRIT)
TATTA (THP)
?
WE'RE HERE TO FIND OUT WHERE TO MEET WITH CIRCUS!
ONCE WE FIND THEM, WE'LL ASK THEM ABOUT KAROKU, REMEMBER!?
DON'T TALK LIKE YOU'RE NOT INVOLVED IN THIS!

BUT THE MAN TOLD US TO WAIT FOR HIM...

HI.

HE'S JUST A COMPANY SECURITY GUARD OR SOMETHING.

NSHO (SQUISH)

IF THE PEACE-KEEPERS RECOGNIZE YOU HERE, IT'LL ALL BE OVER.

IGNORE WHAT HE SAID!

SIR...

にっこり

NIKKORI (SMILE)

I'M TERRIBLY SORRY MY SUBORDINATE WASN'T ABLE TO GUARD YOU SUCCESSFULLY.

SHE WAS A GREAT HELP. SHE PRIORITIZED MY GRAND-DAUGHTER'S SAFETY AT ALL TIMES, AS I ASKED.

ELISKA, GO WAIT IN THE CAR, PLEASE.

MAY I TAKE A MOMENT OF YOUR TIME?
I'D LIKE TO ASK YOU A FEW QUESTIONS YOUR MEN WEREN'T ABLE TO ANSWER FOR ME...
I WOULD TRULY LOVE TO, BUT...
DEAR ME...

I'VE BEEN EXPERIENCING SOME CHEST PAIN—VERY LIKELY DUE TO THIS STRESSFUL SITUATION.
...I'M GETTING ON IN YEARS...
FORGIVE ME, MY PHYSICIAN'S HERE TO EXAMINE ME. SO IF YOU'LL EXCUSE ME...
I'VE SENT MISS ELISKA HOME AHEAD OF US.
OH MY.
I CAN SEE SOME CLEAR SIGNS OF FATIGUE. IT MUST HAVE BEEN QUITE AN ORDEAL.
YES... I ALLOWED MYSELF TO BE CAPTURED ON PURPOSE SO I COULD SEE *THOSE TWO* IN ACTION MYSELF...
BUT THE SLANDEROUS ABUSE OF THOSE MISERABLE WORMS WAS SO TIRESOME, IT MADE ME WANT TO VOMIT.
YOU SHOULD LIMIT YOUR FUN A BIT, YOU KNOW.
YOU CAN ALWAYS PUT ME IN PLAY IF THE NEED ARISES.

THAT REMINDS ME—I ENCOUNTERED SOMEONE WHO INTERESTS ME.
IT SEEMS HE HAS UNUSUAL HEARING ABILITY.
I CAN'T SAY QUITE HOW, BUT SOMETHING ABOUT HIM REMINDS ME OF *HIM*.
WOULD YOU CAPTURE HIM FOR ME?
HIRATO OF CIRCUS SEEMS TO BE INTERESTED IN HIM TOO.
HIRATO!
IT LOOKS LIKE THOSE TWO ARE GONE.
YES.
THIS IS HIM, ISN'T IT?
SIGH...
THAT LITTLE BOY IS A WANTED FUGITIVE?
TA (THP)
TA
TA

FOR NOW, LET'S FIND A PLACE WE CAN REST UP.
I'M WARNING YOU—DON'T WANDER OFF AND GET SEPARATED FROM ME, GOT IT?
...HEY!
OKAY.
THANK GOODNESS I AT LEAST HAD MY WALLET IN MY JACKET POCKET.
ARE YOU SERI-OUS!?
HE'S GONE!!
THAT LITTLE BRAT! I'M PUTTING HIM ON A LEASH!!
WAUGH!
I'M SO SORRY!
STOP THAT!!
BERO (LICK)
BERO
HA (PANT)
HA
PATA (WAG)
PATA
?
?

Score 4: Circus

It seems you ran into some trouble resolving yesterday's train incident, 2nd Ship Captain Hirato.
Your superior's teaching methods are perhaps too soft.
SAYING THAT RIGHT IN FRONT OF THE SUPERIOR IN QUESTION IS RATHER NASTY OF YOU, ISN'T IT?
1st Ship Captain, it is not your place to speak on this.
I SHALL REFLECT UPON MY MISMANAGE-MENT AND ENSURE IT DOES NOT HAPPEN AGAIN.
Very well. You may go now.
WHAT A NOISY BUNCH! GEEZERS GET SO SET IN THEIR WAYS, THEIR MINDS JUST CRUST RIGHT OVER!
AND WHY DID YOU NEED TO TAG ALONG?
I THOUGHT IT'D BE FUN TO SEE HOW YOU LOOK WHILE GETTING CHEWED OUT...
NEXT TIME WE MEET IN THE SKIES, I'M PUMPING YOU FULL OF LEAD!

Tooji, the Bay City
A "SHOW"?
YOU DON'T KNOW ABOUT THE SHOWS!?
WHENEVER CIRCUS DOES A BIG OPERATION TO CATCH SOME BAD GUYS...
...THEY PUT ON A SHOW FOR THE TOWNSPEOPLE AS AN APOLOGY FOR PUTTING US THROUGH SUCH A SCARY THING.
THAT'S WHY, EVEN WHEN I CAN'T PLAY OUTSIDE BECAUSE CIRCUS IS CHASING BAD GUYS...
...I NEVER GET SAD. ♡
IS THERE SOMEONE NAMED KAROKU IN CIRCUS?
HUUUUH? I DON'T KNOW... BUT THERE ARE LOTS OF CIRCUS SHIPS.
THERE'S A SHIP IN TOWN RIGHT NOW. THEY WERE DOING AN OPERATION THROUGH THE NIGHT BEFORE LAST!
KANA!
OH!
I'VE GOTTA GO.
THANK YOU FOR ALWAYS WATCHING HER!
THANK YOU FOR THE YUMMY FRUIT!
LET'S GO, NAI.

PEN (SMOOSH)
AND STOP LOSING YOUR CAP, GOT IT!?
A WANTED FUGITIVE CAN'T GO AROUND BLATANTLY SHOWING HIS FACE!
YOU DO GET THAT YOU'RE BEING PURSU—
HA (GASP)

GO (BAM)

FUWARI (FWOOF)

WE'RE PEACEKEEPERS!

THERE'S MORE OF THEM AROUND. MUST BE BECAUSE OF THE "SHOW"...

GAREKI... CAN'T BREATHE...

SUPPORI (SQUISH)

...BUT ANYWAY, HOW LUCKY IS IT THAT THE TOWN WE CHOSE TO START OUR SEARCH FOR CIRCUS IN WOUND UP HAVING A CIRCUS SHIP VISITING IT?

MAYBE THE ONE THING YOU'VE GOT GOING FOR YOU IS STRONG LUCK, HUH?

TON (TAP)

BY THE WAY...

...HAVE YOU HEARD THAT SOUND AGAIN?

SOUND?

THE SOUND YOU KEPT HEARING WHILE WE WERE ON THE TRAIN...
...UH.

HEY...
ARE YOU LISTENING...?
JII (STARE)
PI (TWEET)
PI
THAT REMINDS ME...
ON THE TRAIN...
......
...WE FOUND THE BOMBS HIDDEN RIGHT WHERE HE SAID HE HEARD A NOISE.
THAT GOES BEYOND JUST STRONG LUCK.

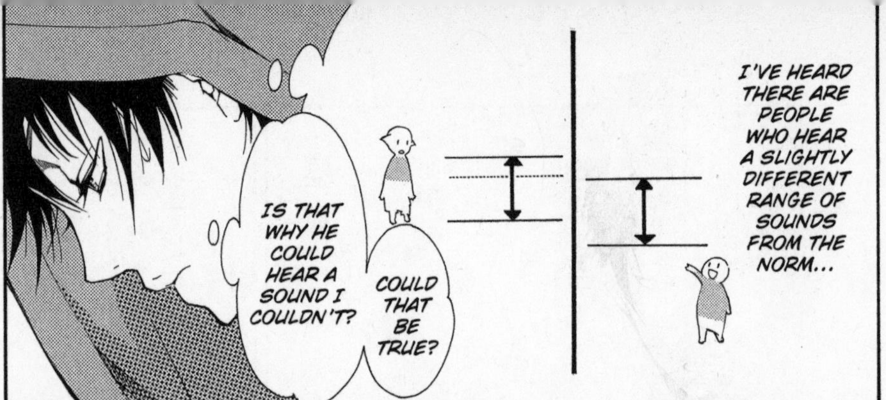
I'VE HEARD THERE ARE PEOPLE WHO HEAR A SLIGHTLY DIFFERENT RANGE OF SOUNDS FROM THE NORM...
COULD THAT BE TRUE?
IS THAT WHY HE COULD HEAR A SOUND I COULDN'T?

WELL, WHATEVER...
AH, WELCOME BACK.
HOW DID IT GO TODAY?

WHEN WE GO TO CIRCUS AND SEE KAROKU...
...I WONDER IF HE'LL TELL ME WHY HE WENT AWAY ALL OF A SUDDEN.
AND THEN, THE BRACELET.
I'LL ASK RIGHT AWAY IF I CAN GIVE IT TO YOU!

THANKS.

YOU MAY GET TO SOON, SINCE WE'LL BE ABLE TO MEET UP WITH REAL CIRCUS MEMBERS AT THE SHOW TONIGHT.

WE'LL LOOK FOR SOMEONE IN CHARGE.

SO DON'T GO OUT ON YOUR OWN!

IF YOU GET CAUGHT BY THE PEACE-KEEPERS, YOU WON'T GET TO SEE KAROKU.

IF THE AREA WE RAN INTO THOSE PEACE-KEEPERS EARLIER IS WHERE THEY EXPECT THE BIGGEST CROWDS...

...THE BEST ROAD TO TAKE TO THE PLAZA WHERE THE SHOW IS BEING HELD IS...

TON TON (TAP)

HEY...

WHEN YOU MEET CIRCUS, WILL YOU BE ABLE TO EXPLAIN WHO YOU ARE TO THEM?

UM... ......

"I'M ..."

"... NAI."

NO.

STOP

NEVER MIND, I'LL DO IT.

"IT SEEMS LIKE THIS KID WAS LIVING IN A FOREST TO THE WEST OF KARASUNA WITH HIS OLDER BROTHER.

"BUT HIS BROTHER VANISHED ONE DAY, AND ALL THAT COULD BE FOUND OF HIM WERE SOME BLOODSTAINS."

THAT'S WHY, EVEN IF HE'S GONE NOW...
...THIS TIME, I WANT TO DO THAT FOR HIM.
AH...
OKAY.
I DON'T REALLY GET IT.
NOT THAT IT MATTERS.
DON (BOOM)
PIII (FWEEEET)
CIRCUS'S SHOW IS STARTING! IT'S SO PRETTY!
THE TENSION IN THE AIR DURING THE OPERATION IS TOTALLY GONE NOW!
WOW! THE WHOLE TOWN LOOKS SO DIFFERENT!
THERE WAS A DIFFERENT MONSTER OVER THERE!
LET'S GET TO THE TENT FIRST!

GAREKI!
THERE!
WOW...
THIS WAY, COME ON!!
...!
BOFUU (BOMMF)
OH MY, LITTLE BOY.
SORRY ABOUT THAT.
HEY, WHAT ARE YOU DOING? DON'T WANDER OFF...
MISTER!
MISTER!
GUI (GRIP)

GET FOR THAT ME! ...
......
PASHII (VOOSH)
ぱしいっ
AH!
DON'T RELY SO EASILY ON OTHERS.
AND DON'T GRAB THEM.
GYUUUU (SQUEEEZE)
IF YOU LET GO OF YOUR BALLOON, YOU LOSE IT. GOT THAT?
うわあああんっ
WAAAAAH!
HNGH!
HNGH!
......
GUN (PULL)
OH MY! WHAT A NICE YOUNG MAN.
!?
GAREKI'S AMAZING ...
I RESPECT HIM...

NAI?
MA...
HUH?
MAAAA MAAAA!
WAAAAAH!
UM...
WAAAAAUGH!
WAH!
UH...
HNNGH!
ORO (PANIC) ORO ORO
WAH! WAH!
ARE YOU OKAY...?
WAAAH!
PON (TAP)
HEY, THERE...
IS THIS LITTLE GIRL LOST?

THE PEACE-KEEPERS WILL TAKE CARE OF HER.
IF YOU GET CAUGHT BY THE PEACEKEEPERS, YOU WON'T GET TO SEE KAROKU.
HA (GASP)
はっ
UH...
UM...
WELL ...
OZU (NERVOUS)
おず
PLEASE ...
...TAKE CARE OF HER...
GYUU (GRIP)
ぎゅう...
HUH?
ARE YOU...
THAT FACE...!
DOPYUU (DOINK)
どぴゅーっ
HEY!
WAIT !!
MAMA...

THIS IS SECTOR B!
I'VE FOUND THE BOY FUGITIVE!
WAH!
GOODNESS!
NO RUNNING HERE!
STOP RIGHT THERE!
CANDY BARS!
DOGOO (WHUMP)
AWA AWA (FRANTIC)
GYUMUU (SMOOSH)
OH! PARDON ME!
THE MASCOT...
IS SHE DEAD?
HEY...
...
HEY! STOP, I SAID!
PU (BOOP)
PUU
PUU

ピ
PI (BEEP)
IT'S ME.
Sir, we've confirmed the boy's location.
I SEE.
BRING HIM HERE AND MAKE SURE HE'S NOT DAMAGED.
ROGER.
THAT IDIOT ...!
NAI!

どん
DON (BUMP)
AH! SORRY ...
IT'S OKAY ...

きゃわ
きゃわ
KYAWA KYAWA (MURMUR)

NAI!
!!

NAI!

GAREKI ...!
!

WAH!
WAAAH!
ぱああああ
PAAAAA (FWAAAAA)

WHOA!
WHAT THE...
SA (HOP)
どおっ
DOO (BAM)
HUH? DO YOU KNOW WHERE MY HEAD WENT?
I ONLY PUT IT DOWN FOR A SECOND...
NO CLUE.
YOU...
... LITTLE ...!!
YOU WANDERED OFF AND GOT SPOTTED BY THE PEACE-KEEPERS!?
PUT THAT ON!!
PUNISHMENT FOR WANDERING OFF.
JIN (THROB)
じんじん
JIN
PUNISHMENT FOR BEING SEEN BY THE PEACEKEEPERS.
あわ
AWA (PANIC)
あわ
AWA
MAKE SURE YOU ZIP IT ALL THE WAY TO THE TOP!!
LET'S GO!!
ぐいっ
GUN (PULL)

POON
(FLIP)
わあああ
WAAAA
(WOOOOW)

ISN'T CIRCUS GREAT?
SO PRETTY!
IT LOOKS LIKE BOTH THE SHOW SPECIALISTS AND OPERATIONS SPECIALISTS...
...PUT ON THE SHOW TOGETHER!
THE OPERATION THEY CONDUCTED TWO NIGHTS AGO WAS TO CATCH A DRUG RING!
I SAW IT ALL FROM MY WINDOW!

SHE LOOKS LIKE A LITTLE DOLL!
JUST LIKE YOU IN YOUR YOUNGER DAYS, DEAR.
IT WAS REALLY COOL! THEY USED A STREET BLOCKADE TO TRAP THE RING!
BUT THEY DIDN'T WARN US, SO I GOT PRETTY SCARED.
THE CROOKS WOULD'VE RUN IF THEY DID THAT!
AND WHO CARES? THEY THREW US THIS AWESOME FESTIVAL AFTERWARD.

I—
I'M SORRY TO BOTHER YOU. I'M FROM THE PEACE-KEEPERS.
BISHI (SALUTE)

I RECEIVED A REPORT FROM MY SUPERIORS.
THE FUGITIVE WAS SPOTTED IN THIS AREA, BUT...
KACHI (SQUIRM)
KOCHI (SQUIRM)
I WONDER IF I CAN ASK FOR A PHOTO WITH HER...
KAA (BLUSH)
...I REGRET TO REPORT THAT WE'VE LOST SIGHT OF HIM.

Send me, Hirato.
YOU'RE IN THE MIDDLE OF A SHOW.
YOU NEED TO ENTERTAIN THE TOWNSFOLK.
PI (BEEP)
Yes...
It's me, Yogi...
WHAT IS IT?
YOU SOUND UPSET.
Y...
You won't believe what just happened!! A boy crashed into me from behind without apologizing, and then this peacekeeper came—
—and totally stomped all over me!
DID EVERYONE HEAR THAT?
WHO'S NEAR SECTOR N-11 RIGHT NOW?
GO SECURE THE BOY IN QUESTION AND THE DARK-HAIRED YOUTH WITH HIM.
FU (VWIP)
Wait, are you listening to me!? Hirato!!

ACCORDING TO THE MAP, THIS IS THE FASTEST ROUTE TO THE REAR OF THE FAIRGROUNDS...
THE PEACEKEEPERS WOULDN'T EXPECT A FUGITIVE TO RUN STRAIGHT TO A FAIRGROUNDS WHERE CIRCUS WAS!
THE PEACEKEEPERS WOULD GO IN THE COMPLETE OPPOSITE DIRECTION.
I SHOULD BE ABLE TO SHAKE THEM HERE...
HA (GASP)
SU (FWOOP)

BACHII (BZZZZ)
N!?
GAREKI!!
HEY.
IT'S THIS KID.
UH ...
DOSAA (FWUMP)
PARI (CRACKLE)
ALL RIGHT! THE TASER WORKED.
WH ... AT ...
HUH? THAT KID?
LEAVING THAT ONE'LL BE TROUBLE-SOME. KILL HIM.
OW! YOU LITTLE BRAT!
I CAN'T MOVE... WHO ARE THESE GUYS...?
THIS IS BAD...
HOLD IT.
WHAT DO YOU THINK YOU'RE DOING?

FROM THE NATIONAL SUPREME DEFENSE FORCE "CIRCUS"...
...I AM YOGI, 2ND SHIP COMBAT SPECIALIST!
READY FOR ACTION!

...CIRCUS!?
NOW, THEN. I'LL HAPPILY BE YOUR OPPONENT.
WHO'LL STEP UP TO FACE ME?
OR WILL YOU BOTH FACE ME AT ONCE?
......
...!
AH?
PYUU (ZOOM)

THANK GOODNESS! I GET NERVOUS THE SECOND I START A BATTLE!
KAA (BLUSH)
OH!
BA (WHIRL)
YOU TWO!
BIKUU (STARTLE)

WE MET THIS MORNING, DIDN'T WE?
I WAS IN THE FUR SUIT, SEE?
WAS IT FATE?
YOU'VE GOT...THE WRONG GUYS...

BUT HOW ODD... YOU'RE NOT HOW I IMAGINED YOU AT ALL...
WANTED MURDERERS...
HMMM...

THAT...
WELL, NEVER MIND THAT.
SUKU (RISE)
PI (BEEP)
PI
PI
PARI (CRACKLE)
GU (RAISE)

I WAS TOLD TO BRING YOU GUYS IN.
SO COME WITH ME FOR NOW, OKAY?

THIS IS YOGI.
WHAT?
BRING THEM UP NOW?
THAT SURE WAS FAST!
CIRCUS WAS LOOK-ING FOR US ...?
GOON (RUMBLE)
GOON
WHAT DOES THAT MEAN?

WELL! SHALL WE BE OFF!? ♡
WELCOME TO OUR CIRCUS SHIIIIP!

Score 5: Black Sheep

WELCOME BACK-BAA.
WELCOME BACK-BAA.
I'M HOME.

Score 5: Black Sheep

TWO TEMPORARY GUESTS, HERE TO VISIIIT! ♡
I CAN STAND ... SO ...
WELCOME BACK-BAA.
WELCOME BACK-BAA.
YOU TWO SHOULD SAY "I'M HOME" TO THEM TOO!
I'M HOME!

TRY IT!
I'M HOME ...
Voice prints registered.
キュイイィーン
KYUIIIN (WHIIIR)

STARTING NEXT TIME, IF YOU DON'T REPLY WITH "I'M HOME" TO THEM...

...THEY'LL CHASE YOU OUT OF THE SHIP.

I'M GLAD TO SEE YOU AGAIN.
I WAS RATHER HURT THAT YOU ABANDONED ME WHEN I ASKED YOU TO WAIT.
BUT I'VE TAKEN THE TIME TO LEARN ABOUT YOU.
YOU'VE MET?
THIS GUY...
YOU'RE GAREKI-KUN AND NAI-KUN, CORRECT?
PLEASE HAVE A SEAT.
THE GUY FROM THE TRAIN...!

NOW, THEN.
ALLOW ME TO REINTRODUCE MYSELF.

I AM THE CAPTAIN OF THE 2nd SHIP OF THE NATIONAL SUPREME DEFENSE FORCE "CIRCUS"...
... HIRATO.

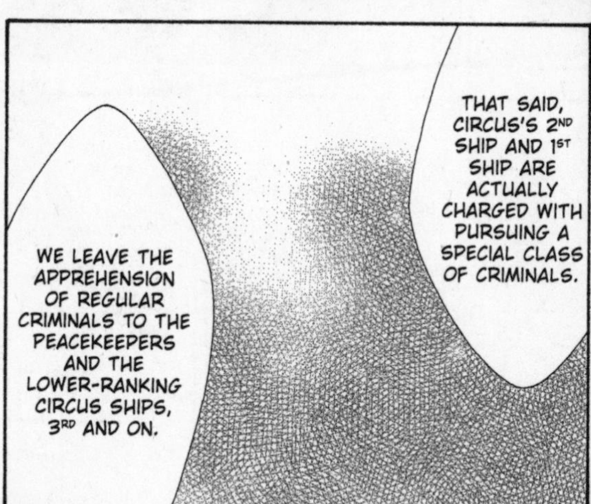
I AM ONE OF THE FEW AUTHORIZED TO APPREHEND PERPETRATORS OF HOMICIDE.

THAT SAID, CIRCUS'S 2nd SHIP AND 1st SHIP ARE ACTUALLY CHARGED WITH PURSUING A SPECIAL CLASS OF CRIMINALS.
WE LEAVE THE APPREHENSION OF REGULAR CRIMINALS TO THE PEACEKEEPERS AND THE LOWER-RANKING CIRCUS SHIPS, 3rd AND ON.

ABOUT NAI'S CRIME —
AH.
WAIT A MOMENT.

I HAVEN'T FINISHED SPEAKING YET.
JUMPING TOPICS TOO QUICKLY MAKES ONE APPEAR RASH.
IT ISN'T CHARMING AT ALL.
NAI-KUN.
AH...
REGARDING THE MURDER CHARGES AGAINST YOU, I INVESTIGATED YOUR CASE PERSONALLY AND FOUND POSITIVE PROOF THAT YOU ARE INNOCENT.
WE NEEDN'T GO ON ABOUT A MATTER THAT'S RESOLVED.
MORE IMPORTANTLY, THERE IS SOMETHING I WISH TO CONFIRM ABOUT THE ITEM THAT STARTED THIS ENTIRE MATTER.
THE ITEM YOU CARRY WITH YOU.
HUH?
REALLY? YOU SHOULD HAVE TOLD US SOONER, HIRATO!
YOU HAVE A CIRCUS ID?

ぱっ
BA (VWA)
UM ...!
IS KAROKU HERE ...!?
HE DROPPED THIS AND NEVER CAME BACK!
WHEN HE DISAPPEARED...
...THERE WAS RED WATER... I MEAN, THERE WAS BLOOD... YES, BLOOD... ALL THE WAY TO THE SEA...
NAI...
HE ACTUALLY LEARNED THE WORD "BLOOD," THEN?
THIS BELONGS TO CIRCUS, SO I WANTED TO COME AND ASK YOU ABOUT IT.
AND GAREKI CAME TOO...
...YOU ARE...
...INCORRECT.

HUH?
BUT WHAT YOU HOLD IS INDEED A CIRCUS ID.
IT'S ABOUT A GENERATION BEHIND THE IDS WE CURRENTLY USE, HOWEVER.
......
FIRST OF ALL, THERE IS NO ONE BY THE NAME OF KAROKU IN CIRCUS.
!!
WELL, THERE'S NO NEED TO BE SO DISAP-POINTED.
WHAT WE KNOW IS THAT AN ITEM THAT SHOULD HAVE BEEN DESTROYED SOMEHOW ENDED UP OUTSIDE THE AGENCY.
THIS IS A MATTER WE MUST GET TO THE BOTTOM OF AND STOP IF NECESSARY.
WOULD YOU BE WILLING TO HELP US?

IT SEEMS LIKELY YOU'D FIND A CLUE FOR WHAT YOU SEEK IF YOU TOOK THIS PATH.
O—
OKAY!
GAREKI-KUN.
NAI...
YOU KNOW OF A WOMAN NAMED MINE, DON'T YOU?
WHAT MAKES YOU THINK YOU DESERVE TO LIVE?

!

DID YOU THINK YOU HAD KILLED A CIRCUS MEMBER?

I HAVE NO IDEA WHAT YOU MEAN.

I TOLD YOU I DON'T KNOW THIS PERSON.

I WAS IMPRESSED BY THE EXPERTISE WITH EXPLOSIVES YOU DISPLAYED ON THE TRAIN.

IN THE WRECKAGE OF MINE'S MANSION, WE FOUND TRACES OF EXPLOSIVES AS WELL.

BASED ON THOSE, I EXPECT THEY WERE MADE BY SOMEONE RATHER KNOWLEDGE-ABLE ABOUT BOMBS AS WELL...

I'VE INVESTIGATED YOU TOO, GAREKI-KUN.

IN ADDITION TO YOUR WORK AS A DAY LABORER, YOU HAVE A RING WITH WHICH YOU COMMIT BURGLARIES, DON'T YOU?

......

THIS GUY... HOW MUCH DOES HE KNOW?

YOUR TARGETS ARE ALWAYS RICH PEOPLE WHO HAVE COME UPON THEIR FORTUNES BY ILL-BEGOTTEN MEANS. THAT'S YOUR OWN SENSE OF MORALITY, I SUPPOSE?

IT SEEMS YOU'VE ACCUMULATED QUITE A BIT OF MONEY.

URGH...

WHAT IS IT THAT YOU NEED SO MUCH MONEY FOR?

UM... GAREKI...

...GAVE ME FOOD AND BOUGHT ME A TRAIN TICKET...

...AND EVEN THIS HAT...

I THINK...
URK...
...HE USED MONEY FOR THOSE THINGS...

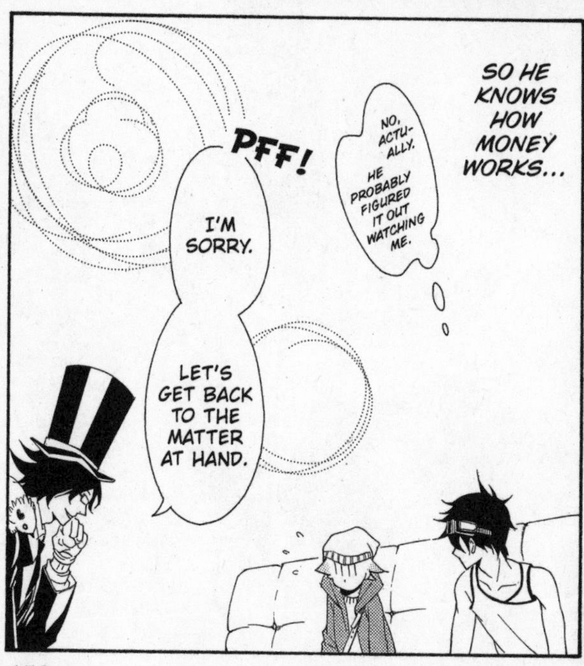

SO HE KNOWS HOW MONEY WORKS...
NO, ACTUALLY. HE PROBABLY FIGURED IT OUT WATCHING ME.
PFF!
I'M SORRY.
LET'S GET BACK TO THE MATTER AT HAND.

I DO NOT INTEND TO FILE A CASE AGAINST GAREKI-KUN.
AS I MENTIONED, REGULAR CRIMINALS ARE NOT IN MY JURISDICTION.
AND THE INFORMATION YOU CAN PROVIDE IS FAR MORE VALUABLE TO ME.
YOU HAD THE GREAT MISFORTUNE OF RUNNING INTO MINE...
...WHO WAS ONE OF OUR MOST WANTED CRIMINALS.
HUMANS WITH HORRIFIC BODIES WARPED IN THE NAME OF "EVOLUTION" LIKE HER...
...ARE THE CLASS OF CRIMINALS WE HUNT.

GAREKI-KUN...
DURING YOUR FIGHT WITH MINE ...
...YOU WEREN'T DOUSED BY ANY OF HER BLOOD, WERE YOU?
THESE BEINGS ARE SENSITIVE TO THE SCENT OF THEIR KIND'S BLOOD.
IF YOU WERE HIT, THERE'S A CHANCE MANY OF THEM WILL COME AFTER YOU.
SO FOR NOW, YOU WILL REMAIN HERE.
FORGIVE ME, BUT YOU HAVE NO RIGHT TO DECLINE.
ALL RIGHT?
TOO HEAVY!
THIS ATMOSPHERE'S TOO HEAVY!!
ARGH ...
UWAHN!

COME ON!
YOU'RE SPEAKING SO FORMALLY TOO!
JUST LISTENING TO YOU IS TIRING ME OUT!
WHY ARE YOU BEING SO STIFF, HIRATO?
SINCE WE'RE GOING TO BE TOGETHER FOR A BIT, LET'S BE MORE FRIENDLY!
FRIENDLY!
OH?
YOU WERE IN HERE, YOGI?
I FORGOT ...
HUH!?
がーん
GAAN (SHOCK)
AH.
ONE THING MORE, GAREKI-KUN.
UGH...
YOU WEREN'T THE ONE WHO KILLED MINE.
DO YOU FEEL RELIEVED AT THAT?
YOU ACTUALLY HATE KILLING, DON'T YOU?
PI (CHIRP)
ピッ
バタン
BATAN (CLANG)
WHA...
I HATE THAT GUY...
MUKAA (GRRR)
ムカア...
...

...
...
I...
...WILL DEFINITELY SEE KAROKU AGAIN.
I WANT TO ASK HIM AS SOON AS POSSIBLE IF I CAN GIVE YOU THE BRACELET.
NAI?
GOON (RUMBLE)
GOON
HEY, YOU TWO! AREN'T YOU HUNGRY?

WE BROUGHT DINNER FROM OUR FOOD SERVERS!
SUDDEN, RADICAL CHANGES IN ONE'S SITUATION CAN CAUSE FATIGUE AND ANXIETY, RESULTING IN THE DETERIORIATION OF YOUR PHYSICAL CONDITION.
SO IT WOULD BE WISE TO EAT AND REGAIN YOUR STRENGTH.
TSUKUMO-CHAN, YOU DON'T HAVE TO BE SO SERIOUS...
THIS SHOULD BE FUN.
HUH?
WHERE'S GAREKI-KUN?
HE'S NOT HERE.
UH ...

GAREKI-KUN!
GAREKI-KUN?
ARE YOU HERE?
GAREKI?
THIS ISN'T GOOD. IT'S EASY TO GET LOST ON THIS SHIP!
I STILL GET LOST SOMETIMES EVEN NOW...
NAI-CHAN, DON'T LEAVE MY SIDE, OKAY?
GU (GRIP)
THE AREA BEYOND IS OFF-LIMITS-BAA.

OH REALLY?
IT'S OFF-LIMITS-BAA.
IT'S OFF-LIMITS-BAA.

I'M JUST TAKING A QUICK LOOK.
DON'T ANY DOORS OPEN OUT?
IT'S OFF-LIMITS-BAA.
IT'S OFF-LIMITS-BAA.
IT'S OFF-
IT'S OFF-LIMITS-BAA.
IT'S OFF-LIMITS-BAA.
IT'S OFF-LIMITS-BAA.
IT'S OFF-LIMITS-BAA.
IT'S OFF-LIMITS-BAA.

SHUT...

...UP ...?
......

BAAAAA!!!

DA (THP)
DA
THAT WAS A PRETTY LOUD BLEATING SOUND JUST NOW ...!

!?

BAAA!
BAAA!
GA...
GAREKI-KUN?
TRESPASSER!
THAT LOOKS LIKE FUN!
BUT IT LOOKS LIKE YOU WANT DOWN, GAREKI-KUN?
BAAA!
TSUN (POKE)
TSUN
BAAA!
BAAA!
BAAA!
BAA!
BAAA!

WAH!?

TRESPASSER.

LET'S GO BACK.

AH ...
NAI-CHAN? WHAT'S WRONG?

NO ...
NOTHING.
I THOUGHT I HEARD SOMETHING...
IT'S JUST THE SHEEP...
NAUSEOUS FROM BEING TOSSED AROUND
ULP!

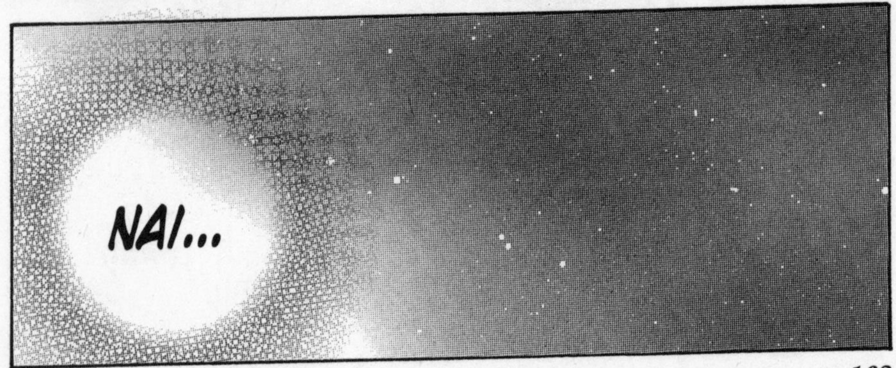

ズル
ZURU
ズル
ZURU (DRAG)
WELL, YOUR SEED SEEMS PRETTY NICE.
BECAUSE IT'S A BLUE ONE.
BLUE FLOWERS WILL GROW FROM THIS.
BUT I...
...HAVE A CERTAIN COLOR I WANT...

GOU (DOOOM)
I HAVE YET...
...TO SEE A RED FLOWER BLOOM!
Gavan, the City of Clay

SCORE 6: Hide-and-Seek

TYPES LIKE GAREKI WHO BELIEVE IN THEIR OWN ABILITIES WILL LIKELY TRY TO RUN OFF ON THEIR OWN QUITE A BIT.
WHICH IS NOT TO SAY I DON'T TRUST THE OTHERS.
AND NAI, ESPECIALLY, NEEDS WATCHING. THERE ARE SEVERAL UNRESOLVED MATTERS ABOUT HIM THAT INTEREST ME.
I CHOSE YOU TWO FOR THIS JOB BASED ON YOUR CHARACTERS.
UNTIL WE ILLUMINATE EVERYTHING SURROUNDING THEM, I'D LIKE TO KEEP THEM CLOSE.
AS FOR THE VARUGA IN GAVAN I MENTIONED EARLIER—

THE FACT THAT HE STARTED HIS ATTACKS ONE TOWN AWAY FROM US MAKES ME THINK...
...NEWS OF GAREKI'S HAVING DEFIED AND BEATEN MINE MAY HAVE GOTTEN OUT ALREADY.
SINCE WE CAN'T BE 100% SURE OF HIS TARGET, WE NEED TO BE ESPECIALLY VIGILANT.
DO YOU UNDER-STAND, TSUKUMO?
...YES.
I APOLOGIZE...
GO (RUMBLE)
GO
GO
GO
GO
GO
GO

BYU
(FWOOOH)
GAREKI
...
SOMETHING JUMPED OUT OF THE SHIP.
HM?
WHERE?
I DON'T SEE ANYTHING.
....
THE SHIP'S DESCEND-ING.

Hey Grace! So the manga was really good and not at all yaoi. The storyline is awesome I think you will really like it!

Love,
Lillian :)

BA (JUMP)
HUH!? GAREKI-KUN!
WHERE ARE YOU GOING?
ARE YOU FEELING BETTER?
WHERE IS THE SHIP LANDING?
I SAW A TOWN FROM THE WINDOW. I'D LIKE TO TAKE A LOOK.
UH, WELL, IT'S ALREADY SO LATE!
ALL THE SHOPS MUST BE CLOSED NOW.
I BROUGHT SOMETHING TO WARM US UP.
SO LET'S ALL HAVE DINNER!
OKAY?

YUMMY!
YEAH, THAT'S THE BEST, ISN'T IT?
THE STICKY OUTSIDE CRUST ON THE HARD-GRILLED RICE IS JUST SO GOOD!
I CAN EAT LIKE FIVE OF THESE!
IT WAS GOOD. THANKS FOR THE MEAL.
IS IT OKAY THAT WE'RE JUST EATING FOR FREE?

OH, SURE THING.
THEN, I'M GONNA GO TAKE A LOOK AT THAT TOWN NOW.
UH!!
SINCE YOU GUYS BROUGHT US ON BOARD PRETTY ABRUPTLY, WE DON'T EVEN HAVE A CHANGE OF CLOTHES.
SOME PLACE'S GOTTA BE OPEN...
CLOTHES! WE HAVE CLOTHES!
WE SPEND MOST OF THE YEAR IN THE AIR, SO WE'VE GOT PLENTY IN STOCK HERE!
YOU CAN PICK WHATEVER YOU LIKE TOMORROW!!

THEN WE'VE GOT NOTHING TO DO.
IT'S TOO EARLY TO GO TO SLEEP RIGHT NOW.
THEN...
...LET'S PLAY HIDE-AND-SEEK!!

...HUH?

AH! BUT GAREKI-KUN MIGHT BE A LITTLE TRAUMATIZED BY THESE GUYS?
I AM NOT.
JIII— (STARE)
THIS SHEEP IS PART OF OUR SHIP'S DEFENSE SYSTEM, SO IT'S GOT SOME AMAZING FUNCTIONS!
RIGHT NOW, I'VE REGISTERED ALL OF US FOR "HIDE-AND-SEEK."
IF YOU HAVEN'T BEEN FOUND AFTER AN HOUR...
...THE SHEEP WILL COME GET YOU!
A KINDLY FUNCTION THAT DOESN'T LET ANYONE WIND UP HIDING ALL ALONE FOREVER!

...

WHO WOULD PLAY THIS?
AND HOW OLD ARE YOU ANYWAY?
I'M TWENTY-ONE IF YOU MUST KNOW.
THERE ARE TIMES WHEN GROWN-UPS WANNA PLAY HIDE-AND-SEEK TOO!!

THEN I'LL BE "IT."
I'M PRETTY GOOD AT IT.
I DOUBT REGULAR PEOPLE COULD COMPETE.
SO FEEL FREE TO STAY OUT OF IT IF YOU WANT.
...

ONE.
TWO.
THREE...
ばっ
BA (RUSH)
HIDE-AND-SEEK...!
かしゃんっ
KASHAN (CLANG)

DO YOU THINK IT'LL BE OKAY?
THE CIRCUS FOLK ARE PRETTY STRONG...
WE'LL BE FINE.
WHAT DO YOU THINK WE BROUGHT ALL THE BODIES TO THE TOWN CENTER FOR?
THEY'LL DEFINITELY COME HERE TO RESCUE THE SURVIVORS.
AND THEN, WE'LL LEAVE THE REST TO *HIM*.
YOGI...
FOUND YOU.
WERE YOU EVEN TRYING ...?
FOUND YOU, GAREKI.
GOOD WORK.
AND HERE I THOUGHT I'D FIND HIM FIRST, BUT...
WHERE'S NAI-KUN?

I MUSTN'T BE FOUND...
I HAVE TO GO SOME-WHERE I CAN'T BE FOUND...
!?
GAKUN (KLANK)
HYU (WOOSH)
WA—WAAAAAAGH!
GORO (TUMBLE)
GORO
GORO
GORO
POOON (POINK)

GURU GURU GURU GURU (ROLL)
ぐるぐるぐる
DOON (DONK)
ドン
OOF ...
GO (DOOOM)

IS THIS ...?
......
HOW FAR DOES THIS SHAFT GO?
UH...?
DARA DARA (DRIP)
OUT-SIDE.
NAI-CHAN!!

ZURU (DRAG)
ZURU
ZURU
ZURU
YOUR ACTIONS AREN'T VERY CONSISTENT.

YOU'RE THE ONE WHO CAME TO ME. SO WHY ARE YOU RUNNING AWAY NOW?
I DON'T KNOW... YOU'RE WRONG ...
NO...

ZAA (WHIZZ)
NO—
GAKIIIN (STAAAB)
PIKON
ピコーン
PIKON (BABEEP)
ピコーン
WAIT...
YOU COULDN'T BE THE...?
Hirato-san

YOGI?
WE'RE TREATING GAVAN'S TOWNS-PEOPLE RIGHT NOW.
OW...
BUT THERE'S SOMETHING ODD ABOUT THE SURVIVORS' WOUNDS.
HELP ME...
There's a good chance the Varuga's true target wasn't them, so be extra-vigilant...
HIRATO-SAN...
YOU'RE A LITTLE LATE.
MY ORDERS ARE TO BRING THAT BOY BACK.
KINDLY STAY OUT OF MY WAY!
BUN (TOSS)
YEEP!?
EYES!!!?
GYAAAH!!

BUWA (WEEEN)
DON (SHOVE)
BA (WEEEEN)
GISHI (WRAP)
UH ...
!
AH...

DO (VWOOP)
HIDE-AND-SEEK IS NOW OVER-BAA.
ONE HOUR HAS PASSED. HAVE YOU BEEN TOLD, "FOUND YOU" YET-BAA?
HUH?
UH...
DOU (ZOOM)

GI (STRAIN)
GI
GI
...!
ACK!
GO (KICK)
ZUGU (THWACK)
GI (CRACK)
GYAAAAAAH!!
BYON (ZWOOP)
HE RAN AWAY ...

NAI-CHAN!!
GAREKI... EVERYONE ...
THANK GOODNESS!
THANK GOODNESS!
WAH!
WAH!
MUAH!
YOU'RE WONDERFUL!
BUCHUU (SMOOCH) ぶちゅ
IT WASN'T ME-BAA. IT WAS HIM-BAA.
LOOKS ANNOYING-BAA.
THAT VARUGA ...
IT SOUNDED LIKE HE WAS SPECIFICALLY TARGETING NAI-KUN FOR A REASON...
I WONDER WHAT IT WAS.
LIKE I'D KNOW.

THAT SUUURE WAS SCARY, HUH~? LET'S GO TAKE A NICE BATH AND WARM UPPP~!
A BA—
KISHI (SKREE)
NAI-CHAN?
GIN (STAB)

AH ...?
AH...
...EA...
...RLY...
ZAZA (FSHHH)
AH...

CAN... YOU...
...HEAR ME CLEARLY...
...NAI?
KA...

KAROKU!

ZAA (RUSTLE)

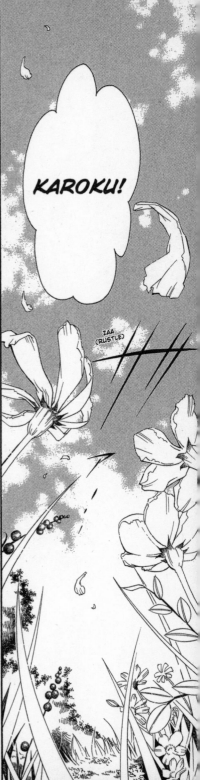

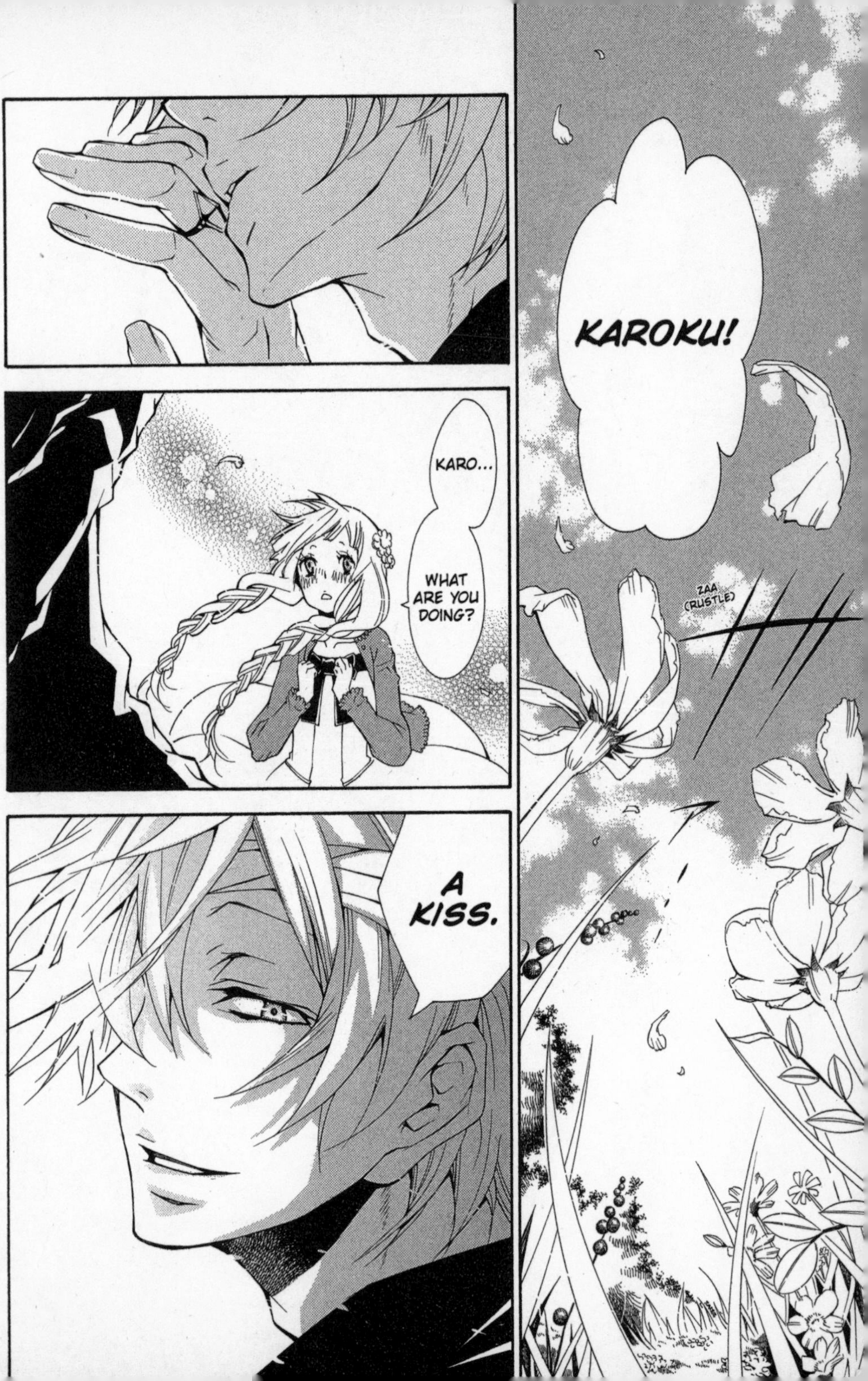

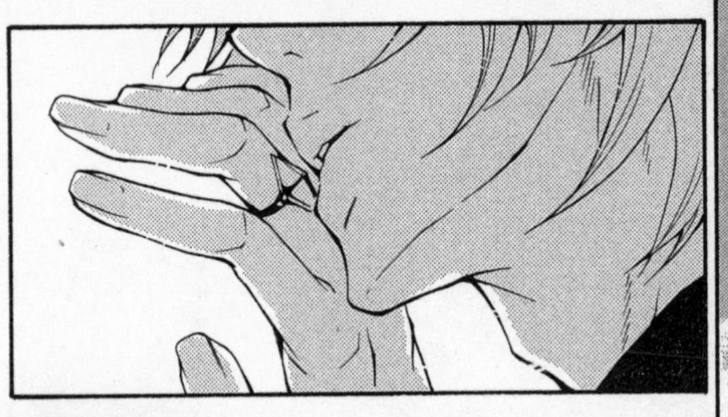

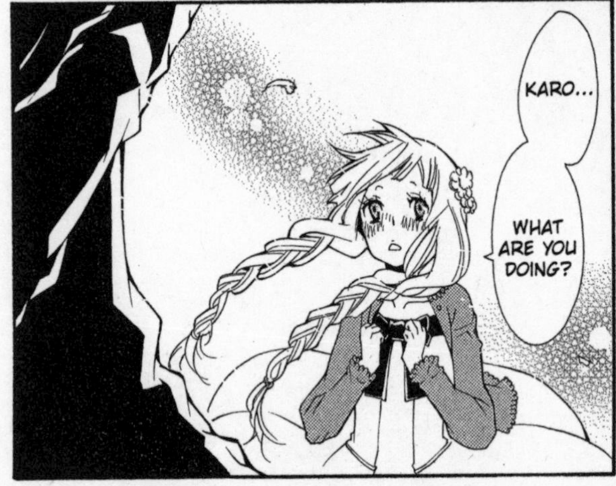
KARO...
WHAT ARE YOU DOING?

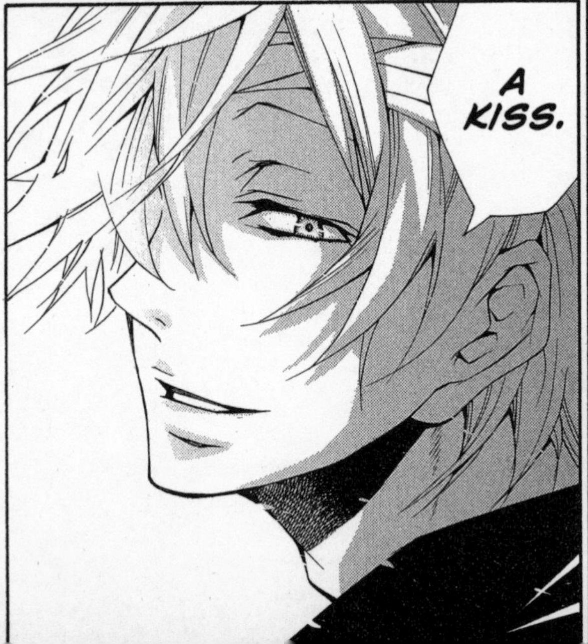
A KISS.

I HEARD YOU WERE CAUGHT UP IN AN INCIDENT...
...ELISKA.
KAROKU ...!

I WAS LONGING TO SEE YOU, KAROKU, SO...
...I PUT UP WITH THE SCARY STUFF...
GYU (HUG)
KAROKU, I WANTED TO SEE YOU...
EE...
AH...
AH!

KARNEVAL

Bonus Comic 1 - "Huh? Listen, you little..."

Bonus Comic 2 - Time ☆ to ☆ Learn!

Bonus Comic 3 - A True Test of Strength ☆

THIS IS ALSO AN IMPORTANT ASPECT OF CIRCUS'S JOB.
DANCE!
(YOGI VERSION)
NERVOUS BEING CENTER OF ATTENTION
OKAY, I'LL PUT ON A SHOW THAT'LL IMPRESS EVERY-ONE! ★
FLY!
THIS IS MY CUTIE MODE! ☆
POP-ULAR WITH KIDS.
WEE! SCARY!
WORK-ING HARD.
SPARKLING BEAM!
WOOOW!
AFTER WORK
DID YOU JUST FINISH WORK TOO, TSUKUMO-CHAN?
OH?
AHH...
GOOD!
WORK!
BACHIIIN (SPARKLE)
DAYYY! ☆
TO!
DUE TO HIS WORK...
...IT'S HABIT?
OR PERHAPS...
...IT'S HIS TRUE SELF?
SHE JOINED CIRCUS AFTER YOGI, SO SHE DOESN'T KNOW FOR SURE.

I'LL BE WAITING FOR YOU IN THE NEXT VOLUME! ♥ LOVE, YOGI

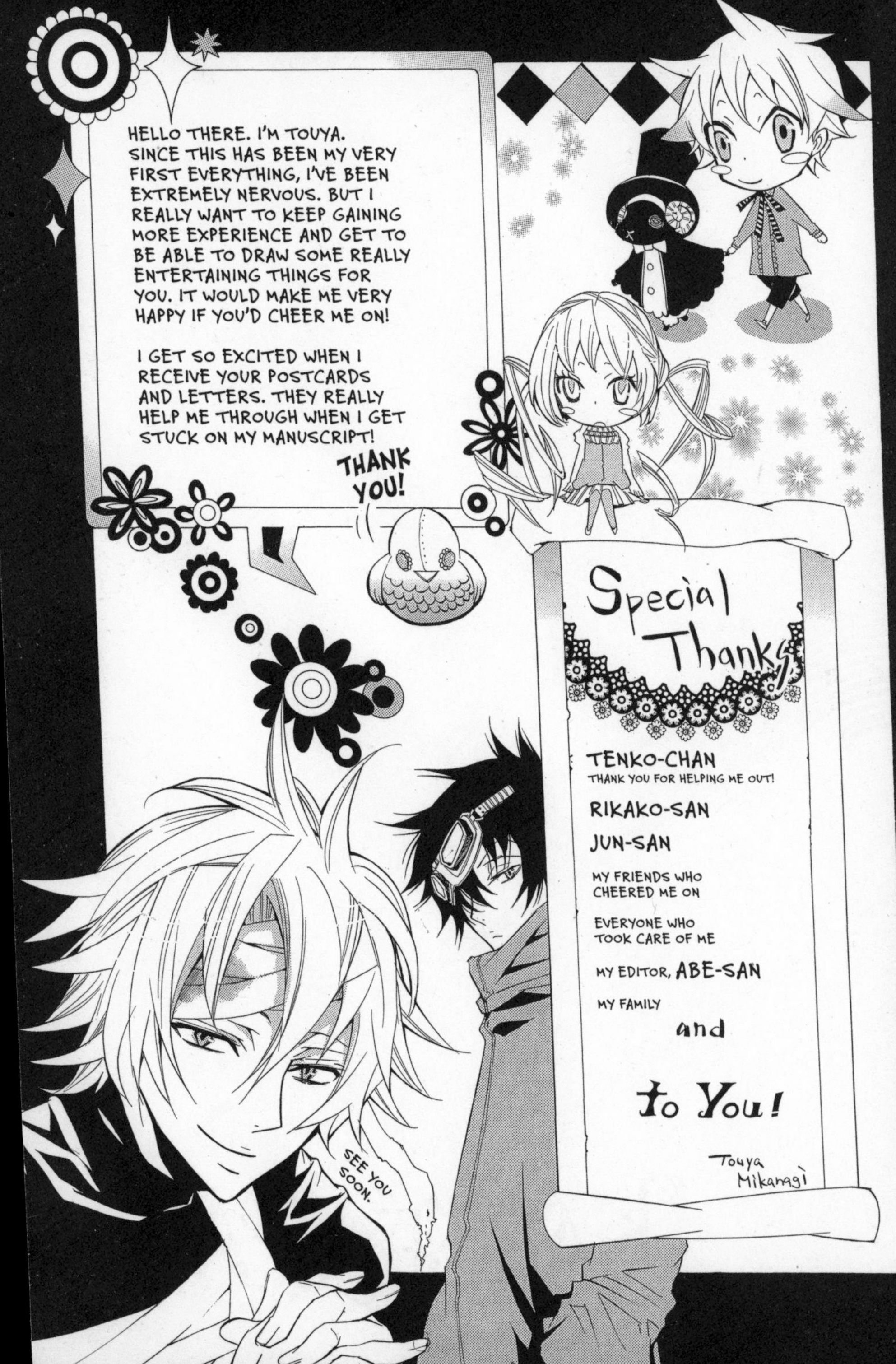
HELLO THERE. I'M TOUYA. SINCE THIS HAS BEEN MY VERY FIRST EVERYTHING, I'VE BEEN EXTREMELY NERVOUS. BUT I REALLY WANT TO KEEP GAINING MORE EXPERIENCE AND GET TO BE ABLE TO DRAW SOME REALLY ENTERTAINING THINGS FOR YOU. IT WOULD MAKE ME VERY HAPPY IF YOU'D CHEER ME ON!
I GET SO EXCITED WHEN I RECEIVE YOUR POSTCARDS AND LETTERS. THEY REALLY HELP ME THROUGH WHEN I GET STUCK ON MY MANUSCRIPT!
THANK YOU!
Special Thanks
TENKO-CHAN
THANK YOU FOR HELPING ME OUT!
RIKAKO-SAN
JUN-SAN
MY FRIENDS WHO CHEERED ME ON
EVERYONE WHO TOOK CARE OF ME
MY EDITOR, ABE-SAN
MY FAMILY
and
to You!
Touya Mikanagi
SEE YOU SOON.

KARNEVAL

KARNEVAL

Score 7: Tears

KAROKU...
I...
I CAME OUT OF THE FOREST BECAUSE I WANTED TO FIND YOU.
THERE ARE SCARY THINGS HERE.
BUT YOU KNOW WHAT? GAREKI...

GAREKI RESCUED ME.
HE ALWAYS STAYED WITH ME AFTER THAT TOO...
IF GAREKI WENT AWAY, I...
...WOULD HAVE BEEN...
...SO LONE—
NAI?

NAI-KUN...!
NAI-CHAN!?
THAT GUY...
GA ...
...HE DIDN'T DO SOMETHING TO YOU, DID HE?
KEEP HIM STILL!!
I'LL GO GET POPS RIGHT NOW!!
HIRATO! NAI-KUN IS...

IT...
...HURTS...
YOU'RE A BOY, AREN'T YOU?
HANG IN THERE.
POOR THING...

...TO HAVE DIED IN PAIN...

GAREKI-KUN?

OH, HOW IS HE!? HOW IS POOR, LITTLE NAI-CHAN!?
POPS! PLEASE, HOW IS HEEE!?
...

THEY'VE GIVEN US THE OKAY TO GO IN. SHALL WE?
POPS!!

GAREKI-KUN, GET DOWN.
WHA?
...ARE YOU... SO ANNOY-ING!!

GET YOUR TOM-FOOLERY OUT OF THE SICK ROOM!!
GASHAAAN (CLAAANG)
CALM YOUR-SELVES!!
THERE'S NOT A SINGLE THING WRONG WITH THE BOY!!
POPS...
...

HOWEVER, THERE WAS AN ODD FLUCTUATION IN HIS BRAINWAVE ACTIVITY BRIEFLY.
IT CAUSED HIM TO LOSE CONSCIOUS-NESS.
I CAN'T DETERMINE THE CAUSE OF THE FLUX FROM HERE UNFORTU-NATELY.
YOU'D BEST TAKE HIM TO THE RESEARCH TOWER FOR FURTHER TESTS.
I SEE. WELL...
TIME IS OF THE ESSENCE, SO I'LL BE OFF.
TAKE THAT FOOL BOY ROLLING AROUND OUTSIDE THE DOOR WITH YOU.
FEEL FREE TO USE HIM FOR HUMAN EXPERIMEN-TATION.
DOC-TOR!

WHEN WILL HE WAKE UP?
I'M RESPONSIBLE FOR THIS.
HE WAS ENTRUSTED TO ME, AND YET—
HIS CONDITION'S STABLE.
HE'LL WAKE UP SOON ENOUGH.

PHEW...
YOU SHOULD BE EASIER ON YOURSELF, TSUKUMO.
YOU DON'T NEED TO SHOULDER BURDENS THAT ARE NOT YOURS.

...!
I'LL HEAD BACK NOW...!
PLEASE TAKE CARE OF NAI-KUN!
NOW, THEN.
WHO MIGHT YOU BE?

HE WAS IN THAT MUCH PAIN, AND NOTHING'S WRONG WITH HIM?
YOU SURE YOU'RE NOT A QUACK?
HOH HOH!
CERTAINLY A HIGH-SPIRITED BRAT, AREN'T YOU?
YOU'RE WORRIED FOR YOUR FRIEND, EH?
HOW'D YOU TWO PAIR UP?
WE'RE JUST INCIDENTAL COMPANIONS.
WHO NEEDS A DUMB THING LIKE FRIENDS?
YOU WON'T HAVE ANY BEAUTIFUL "FATEFUL ENCOUNTERS" LIKE THAT.
NOT WITH THAT PERSONALITY!
YOU'VE GOT ARRESTED DEVELOPMENT, HAVEN'T YOU?
EITHER THAT OR YOU'VE GONE SENILE.

YOU'RE AN INTERESTING FELLOW.
FATEFUL ENCOUNTERS ALWAYS SEEM INCIDENTAL OR MERE COINCIDENCE AT THE START.
BUT IF TRUST WERE TO GROW BETWEEN YOU...
...THAT WOULD BE THE START OF AN ETERNAL FRIENDSHIP.
...HEY! WHERE ARE YOU GOING?
FOR A MID-NIGHT SNACK.
I'M HUNGRY NOW.
WHAT♡ SHALL I EAT?
GUUUUUU (GRUMBLE)
ぐぅぅ
BE SURE TO WATCH HIM ATTEN-TIVELY!
HUH!?

NAI...
WHY AREN'T YOU FOCUSED ON ME?
IS SOMEONE BESIDE YOU?

KAROKU!?
WHERE ARE YOU!?
WHAT KIND OF PERSON IS IT?
UH...
IT'S GAREKI ...
I'M NOT SURPRISED YOU WERE ABLE TO MAKE A FRIEND. YOU'RE MY SON, AFTER ALL.
BUT...
LET'S SAY GOOD-BYE TO HIM, OKAY?

WHOA.
THAT SCARED ME...
HEY...
HOW'RE YOU FEELING?
IF THERE'S SOME-THING YOU WANT ME TO DO FOR YOU...
...JUST THIS ONCE, I'LL DO IT.
GA—
HO (RELIEF)
ほ...
YOU DON'T WANT HIM TO GET BRO-KEN, DO YOU?
BIKU (JOLT)
ビクッ...

DON (SHOVE)
"I DON'T NEED YOU, GAREKI."
"I DON'T NEED ..."
HUH?
WHAT ...
...IS THAT SUPPOSED TO MEAN?

HUH ...?
BIKU (FLINCH)
びくっ
I'M... SCARED OF...
YOU'RE SCARED OF ME?
NOW? SERI-OUSLY?
GA...?
...!
GAREKI ...
WHAT'S THAT SUPPOSED TO BE?

ACTING ALL SWEET AND INNOCENT AND DOING WHATEVER'S EASIEST FOR YOU...
SORRY, BUT I HATE PEOPLE LIKE THAT.
YOU'RE GIVING ME WHAT I WANT...
...SO THAT I'LL GO AWAY?
BATAN (SHUT)
GUESS YOU'RE FINE NOW THAT YOU'VE MET UP WITH CIRCUS, HUH?
ZUKIN (PANG)
...?
はた
HATA (PLOP)
HATA
はた

UGH...
WAA
AAAAH...
HIC!
IT...
ガチャ
GACHA (CLACK)
DOCTOR? I JUST...
...WANTED TO THANK YOU FOR YOUR GUIDANCE EARLIER AND...
HIC ...!
NAI-KUN!?
UH ...!
WAAAH!

OW!
OWW ...
UGH ...
GEEZ ... POPS ...
NOSSORI (SLUGGISH)
YOU'RE NOT AN ORDINARY OLD MAN...
...SO HOLD BACK A LITTLE!
YURARI (SWAY)
SOMEONE'S COM—
GA (SHOVE)

WHERE'D THAT BEARDED GEEZER GO...?
HUH?
UM ...?
GAREKI-KUN?
I GUESS HE MEANS DOCTOR?
TELL HIM THAT ROTTEN BRAT IS AWAKE.
SCA-RY!
SURE THING!
SO LET'S ALL JUST CALM DOWN...
SURREN-DERING
IF THAT'S OKAY?

WAAAAAH!
WHAT DO I DO?
HE SAYS NO PART OF HIS BODY HURTS.
SO WHY IS HE CRYING?

I'D LIKE TO GO GET DOCTOR, BUT I CAN'T LEAVE HIM ALONE...
HIRATO... NO, I SHOULDN'T BOTHER HIM WITH THIS.

I'VE GOT IT—YOGI!
ピポパ
SFX: PIPOPA (BEEP-BOOP-BOP)
Oh, hi, Tsukumo-chan!
YOGI, I HAVE A FAVOR...
That really won't be very possible for me just now. See, it's about to become a murder scene over here, so gets to that point.
WHAT... ARE YOU SAYING?

KOTSU (STEP)
KOTSU

ARE YOU IN?
GI (CREAK)
GI
PLEASE COME IN.

YOU'VE GOT TO REST YOUR EYES EVERY NOW AND THEN.
IT'S BECAUSE YOU DON'T THAT YOU'VE ENDED UP NEEDING GLASSES.
IT'S GENETIC. I'VE WORN GLASSES SINCE I WAS A CHILD.
PLEASE SIT DOWN.

ALL OF THIS IS JUST RAW DATA, ISN'T IT?
I ENJOY SEARCHING FOR THINGS LEFT BEHIND ON THE PAGE.
NOW ...
I'M FAIRLY SURE YOU DIDN'T COME HERE FOR A MIDNIGHT SNACK?

NO.
I HAVE SOMETHING TO TELL YOU ABOUT THAT BOY'S BODY.

...WHAT ABOUT "NAI'S BODY"?

......

IS THERE SOME SERIOUS PROBLEM WITH IT?
WELL, LET ME JUST BE BLUNT.

HE ISN'T HUMAN.

HE'S AN ANIMAL.

SCORE 8: Your Body

IT'S NO WONDER YOU'RE SURPRISED.
I WAS SHOCKED MYSELF...

BU (SNORT)
KUH KUH...
BOSO (MUTTER)
WHAT A TERRIBLE SENSE OF HU...
NO, NO, IT'S SIMPLY ...
I CAN HEAR YOU, YOU REALIZE!?

FORGIVE ME... I HAVE ALWAYS BELIEVED THAT NO MATTER HOW ADVANCED YOUR AGE BECAME, YOU WERE THE TYPE WHO WOULD ALWAYS RETAIN HIS WISDOM...
KU (CHUCKLE)
BUT YOUR SENSE OF HUMOR HAS, ALAS, DECLINED SOMEWHAT WITH THE YEARS...
HOW CAN I SAY IT?
YOU MUST CRAFT YOUR WORDS CAREFULLY.
AN ANIMAL... HA!
I DIDN'T CRAFT MY WORDS AT ALL!

UM, WELL...
...I'M GUESSING THE DOCTOR WILL BE IN HIRATO-SAN'S OFFICE, SO...
WHAT IS THIS AURA AROUND GAREKI-KUN RIGHT NOW?
AH... SOUNDS LIKE HE'S HERE, BUT...
YOU'RE MOCKING ME COM-PLETELY!
KII (CREAK)
HE SOUNDS MAD...?
DOC...
PURI (PRICKLE)
ALL RIGHT, THEN!
TAKE A GANDER AT THIS!
PURI

THE ODD RESULTS OF THE TESTS I RAN ON HIS TISSUE SAMPLES ...
ばっ
BA (SHOVE)
...INDICATE A HIGH POSSIBILITY THAT "NAI" IS ACTUALLY THIS!
Scientific Name: Niji
THIS
EH!?
EEEH!?
NO WAY!
...

WOW...
YOU HAVE A TERRIBLE SENSE OF HU—
SERIOUSLY? AN ANIMAL?
DON'T YOU SAY THAT TOO!
DATA DOES NOT LIE!
WAIT, WAIT, IF DOCTOR IS SAYING IT, IT MUST BE...
BUT NAI-CHAN? AN ANIMAL?
WHAAA!?
EEEEH!?
AND WHY ARE YOU HERE IN THE FIRST PLACE!?

AH!
GAREKI-KUN WANTED TO TELL YOU THAT NAI-CHAN IS AWAKE...
IS HE, NOW?
WELL, ALL OF YOU TAKE A LOOK AT THIS!

DATE

WHAT...?
SERIOUSLY...?

!
DOC-
TOR!
HOW'S
HE
DOING?
HE
APPEARS
TO BE
ALL
RIGHT,
BUT...
!

GAREKI!
....
I DON'T... NEED YOU, GAREKI.
I'M SCARED OF...
YOU'RE SCARED OF ME?
NOW?
FUI (TURN)
SERIOUSLY?

...!
しょぼん
SHOBON (DROOP)
......

WHAT'S WRONG?
DID SOMETHING HAPPEN?
WITH WHAT?
NO.

SO HE'S NOT THE SAME THING WE ARE?
THE DATA SAYS HE'S THAT LITTLE ANIMAL...?
HOW AM I SUPPOSED TO JUST ACCEPT THAT DESPITE THE PHYSICAL EVIDENCE!?

AFTER GETTING INVOLVED WITH THESE CIRCUS FREAKS...
...I KNOW THERE ARE HUMANS WHO TURN INTO MONSTERS AND STUFF.

AND IT'S TRUE...

...THAT NAI'S BEHAVIOR...
...HAS ALWAYS BEEN KIND OF WEIRD...

AT LEAST GET YOUR HANDS DIRTY ENOUGH TO PROTECT YOURSELF!
OKAY!
THEN, WHAT?
HAVING NO MANNERS IS A REAL CRIME, DON'TCHA THINK?
GIRI ギギ GIRI (GRIND)
CAN'T BREATHE...! CAN'T BREATHE...!
PASUN (POOMF) PASUN パスンパスン
ALL THIS TIME, I'VE BEEN...
I DON'T NEED YOU, GAREKI!
MUKAA (GRRR) ムッカア・・・
JUST DOING WHAT'S CONVE-NIENT FOR YOU, HUH?
...!
KAAAAA (BLUUUSH) かあああああ
THAT MAKES ME LOOK LIKE A COMPLETE IDIOT!!

WHA ...
WHAT'S WRONG?
I KNEW IT, SOMETHING HAP—
NOTHING HAP-PENED!
GET LOST RIGHT NOW!
WHA ...!?

ゴォン
GOON (VROMM)
ゴォン
GOON

HIRATO-SAN...
WE'RE HEADING TOWARD THE RESEARCH TOWER, AREN'T WE?

YES.
BECAUSE DESPITE APPEARANCES, DOCTOR ISN'T A SILLY, OLD FOOL.
WE SHOULD FOLLOW PROCEDURE AND HAVE THE BOY EXAMINED THOROUGHLY.
CONTACT TSUKITACHI FOR ME AND TELL HIM I'D LIKE TO CONSULT WITH HIM AT THE RESEARCH TOWER.
HUH? WITH ALL OF TEAM ONE?
NO, JUST HIM.

YOU'RE GOING TO DISCUSS NAI-CHAN WITH HIM?
YES.
THAT REMINDS ME—YOU HAVEN'T TAKEN NAI-CHAN'S BRACELET BACK FROM HIM, HAVE YOU?

YOU DIDN'T... HAVE SOME SPECIAL REASON FOR THAT, DID YOU?

NOTHING ESPECIALLY.

I JUST WANTED TO SEE IF THE BRACELET WOULD SHOW A REACTION TO THE BOY.

HUH?

BUT THE BRACELETS WON'T ACTIVATE FOR ANYONE BUT THEIR OWNERS!

NAI-CHAN SAID IT BELONGS TO HIS OLDER BROTHER...

SO?

HE COULD HAVE LIED ABOUT THAT.

NO WAY!
WHAT REASON WOULD HE HAVE HAD TO LIE?
HE MIGHT'VE IF HE WERE WORKING WITH THE ORGANIZATION WE'RE PURSUING.

AS IT IS, WE STILL DON'T KNOW WHY THEY'RE AFTER HIM.
THE TRUTH ABOUT HIS BODY WAS PRETTY SURPRISING TOO...
BUT HE'S ABSOLUTELY, POSITIVELY A GOOD KID! I CAN FEEL IT...

UH!
HEY ...
WHAT ARE YOU GRINNING ABOUT?
YOU'RE THINKING I'M TOO SOFT AGAIN, AREN'T YOU...?
NOT AT ALL.
THIS IS WHY I CHOSE YOU TO GUARD HIM.

YOU'RE VERY GOOD AT LOWERING OTHERS' GUARDS.
DON'T WORRY ABOUT IT.
THESE LITTLE SUSPICIONS ARE ONLY DUE PRECAUTION ON MY PART.
GEEZ, EVERYTHING'S WORK WITH YOU...
YOU CAN PICK WHICHEVER BUNK YOU WANT TO ROLL AROUND IN.
JUST SIT.

CALM DOWN, YOU'RE TALKING TO A LITTLE KID...

OR—TO AN ANIMAL, ACTUALLY...?

HE LOOKS HUMAN NO MATTER HOW I THINK ABOUT IT...

...BUT HE'S AN ANIMAL?

WELL, THERE'S NO NEED TO GET CHOKED UP WITH EMBARRASS-MENT NOW.

MERA (GLOWER)

...HOW COULD YOU SAY THAT YOU'RE SCARED OF ME!!?
!
BURU (TREMBLE)
ぶる
BURU
ぶる
GOT TOO SHY AND WOUND UP SNAPPING IN DEFENSE
SAY IT IN WORDS!!
I...
I'M NOT SCARED OF YOU!
...!
I'M SORRY I GOT ANGRY AND ACTED LIKE AN IDIOT EARLIER...
...BUT AFTER YOU'D BEEN RELYING ON ME AND EVERY-THING...
BUT KAROKU SAID THAT YOU WOULD...
...GET BROKEN ...
...KA-ROKU?

IRA (IRRITATED)
イラ…
WHAT ARE YOU… NEVER MIND. I'LL CONTROL MYSELF AND HEAR YOU OUT TO THE END.
CON-TINUE!
…HE SAID YOU WOULD GET CAUGHT UP AND BROKEN IN THE SCARY THINGS THAT ALWAYS HAPPEN AROUND ME…
…SO IF I DIDN'T WANT YOU TO BREAK, I SHOULD SAY GOOD-BYE TO YOU…
…AND I SHOULD TELL YOU I DIDN'T NEED YOU…
KAROKU TOLD YOU TO SAY THAT…?
HOW AND WHEN DID YOU MANAGE TO TALK…
…WITH THE GUY YOU'VE BEEN SEARCHING DESPERATELY FOR?
JUST NOW…
BEFORE I WOKE UP…

......
HE DOESN'T MEAN HE TALKED TO HIM IN HIS DREAMS, DOES HE?
ROTTEN, LITTLE ANIMAL!

YOU...
I'VE HAD IT WITH YOUR CRAZY—

"SCARY THINGS THAT ALWAYS HAPPEN AROUND ME..."

IF YOU DON'T WANT GAREKI TO GET CAUGHT UP AND BROKEN...

...IN ALL THE SCARY THINGS THAT ALWAYS HAPPEN AROUND YOU, NAI...

...YOU SHOULD TELL HIM YOU DON'T NEED HIM.

...WHEN I STOP AND THINK ABOUT THAT TURN OF PHRASE...

WOULD HE...

...REALLY SAY WORDS LIKE THAT?

ANYWAY, FROM EVERYTHING I'VE SEEN OF HIM SO FAR...

...THERE'S NO WAY HE'D HAVE ENOUGH CALCULATION IN HIM TO HAVE THOUGHT THIS UP HIMSELF.

...?

BUT WAIT—IF HE'S REALLY AN ANIMAL, THEN WHAT DOES THAT MAKE KAROKU ...?
YOU SAID HE WAS YOUR SIBLING, RIGHT?
KAROKU?

SIB... LING?
NOW THAT I THINK OF IT, HE'S NEVER ACTUALLY SAID HIMSELF THAT KAROKU WAS HIS BROTHER.

THEN...

...HOW LONG HAD YOU GUYS BEEN TOGETHER?

... ALWAYS.

IN MORE CONCRETE TERMS.

...!

SO HE REALLY DOESN'T KNOW...

IT'S CLEAR FROM HIS FACE HE DOESN'T. IN FACT, HE DOESN'T EVEN SEEM TO GRASP THE CONCEPT...

OKAY, THEN.

DO YOU HAVE ANY FAMILY OUTSIDE OF KAROKU? OR ANY ACQUAINTANCES?

...?

WHAT...

...HAVE YOU TOLD KAROKU ABOUT ME?

THAT YOU WERE HERE WITH ME...

THAT'S ALL?
THEN WHY WOULD KAROKU TRY TO HAVE NAI DISTANCE HIMSELF FROM ME?

THERE WAS DEFINITELY A SENSE OF MALICE...
...IN THE WORDS HE USED.

AND IF HE'S ABLE TO "TALK" WITH NAI, WHY HAS HE BEEN NEGLECTING HIM UNTIL NOW?

AH!
......

HOW ARE THEY EVEN TALKING ANYWAY?
KA—

IF THAT WAS HOW HE TRIGGERED THE CONVERSATION ...
...THE GUY'S GOT SOME TWISTED TASTES...
HMMPH!
PLUS, HE PICKED A FIGHT WITH ME, DIDN'T HE?
MY IMAGE OF YOU HAS CHANGED PRETTY DRASTICALLY NOW, BIG BROTHER.
GAREKI ...?

FUAAAA (YAWWWN)
ふあああぁぁ
I'M STILL SLEEPY ...
DIDN'T GET ENOUGH SLEEP...
NOOOOO...
WAKE UP-BAA.
GUI GUI
ぐいぐい
GUI (TUG) GUI
ぐいぐい
WAKE UP-BAA.
IT IS WAKING TIME-BAA.
DAN (BAM)
ダンッ
GOKI (CRACK)
ゴキッ
GUH!
GOOD MORNING!
...!
YOGI.
GOOD MO—
IS EVERY-ONE...
YOUR NECK...IS CROOKED ...

Good morning, Hirato-san! ♥
I have a message from the Control Tower. ♥

Two days hence, we will hold an administrative meeting.
Please make preparations to attend. ♥
THERE'S A MATTER I NEED TO ATTEND TO RIGHT NOW.

PLEASE JUST FORWARD THE MEETING'S MINUTES TO ME AFTERWARD—
Uh-uh! ♥

You can't go playing hooky. ♥
It sounds like they want to hear more about the boy in your custody at the meeting. ♥
!

The higher-ups say to go ahead and produce the test results as quickly as possible. ♥
Hon-estly! ♥

HAA (SIGH)

The site of the meeting will be, as always, at the Round Table of Z. ♥

Please have a safe journey here. ♥

Score 9: The Research Tower

DID THE SHEEP GIVE YOU A GENTLE ROUSING THIS MORNING?
WHAT?

NAI AND GAREKI...
...WE'LL TAKE YOU TWO TO OUR RESEARCH TOWER TO BE CHECKED OVER.
YOGI WILL ACCOMPANY YOU.

WHAT ABOUT YOU, HIRATO-SAN?
TSUKUMO AND I WILL MAKE OUR WAY TO THE ROUND TABLE OF Z TO HEAR THE HIGHER-UPS' COMPLAINTS.

BUT I ALREADY TOLD TSUKITACHI-SAN YOU WANTED TO MEET WITH HIM AT THE RESEARCH TOWER...
YOU NEEDN'T WORRY. TEAM ONE HAS BEEN SUMMONED TO Z AS WELL.

WHAT EXACTLY WILL YOU BE "CHECKING" US FOR?

YOU'RE NOT GOING TO EXPERIMENT ON NAI...

...JUST BECAUSE HIS BODY'S A DIFFERENT ANIMAL SPECIES FROM HUMANS, RIGHT?

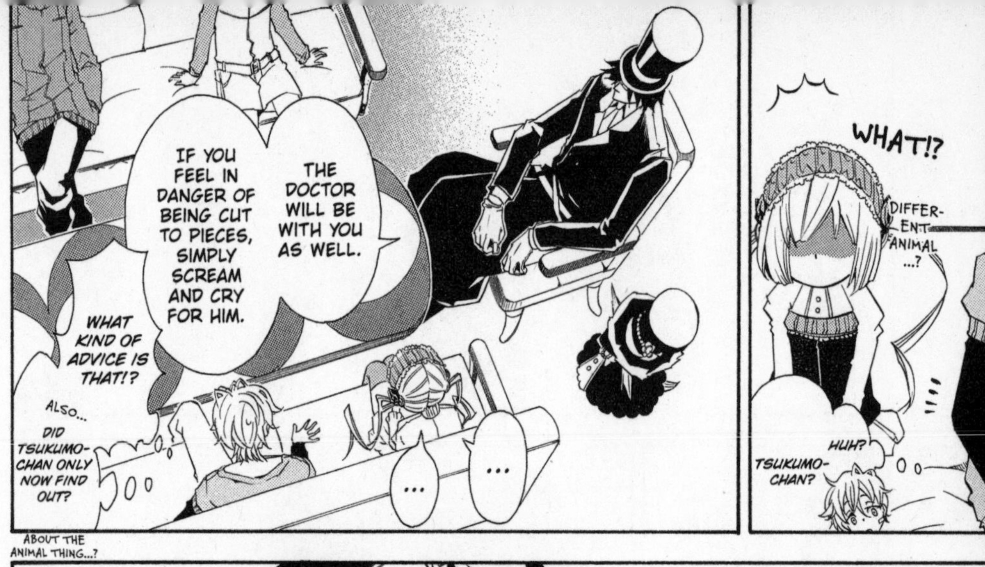

WHAT!?
DIFFERENT ANIMAL...?
HUH? TSUKUMO-CHAN?
THE DOCTOR WILL BE WITH YOU AS WELL.
IF YOU FEEL IN DANGER OF BEING CUT TO PIECES, SIMPLY SCREAM AND CRY FOR HIM.
...
...
WHAT KIND OF ADVICE IS THAT!?
ALSO... DID TSUKUMO-CHAN ONLY NOW FIND OUT?
ABOUT THE ANIMAL THING...?

WELL, IF THEY RESEARCH NAI'S BODY...
...MAYBE THEY'LL BE ABLE TO FIGURE OUT SOMETHING ABOUT KAROKU AND WHY HE WAS WITH HIM...?
I...

...WILL GET...

...THE CHECK-UP!

IF IT WILL TELL US ABOUT KAROKU, I'LL DO ANYTHING!

I SEE.
IF WE LEARN SOME INTERESTING THINGS...
...WE SHOULD BE ABLE TO MAKE SOME MOVEMENTS BASED ON THEM.
HIRATO.
ABOUT NAI-KUN... WHAT WAS THAT ABOUT AN ANIMAL ...?
WHAT?
YOU HAVE AN INTEREST IN TAX-ONOMY?
NO ...
THAT REMINDS ME...
...ACCORDING TO THE BIOLOGY TEXT, HIS NORMAL DIET CONSISTS OF INSECTS.
INSECTS!?
AHHH...
IT REMINDS ME HOW YOU HATED BUGS AS A CHILD. WHAT FUN! IT WAS MY FAULT TOO, IF I RECALL...
NAI-CHAN! GAREKI-KUN!
HOP IN!

HEY!
DOCTOR ...!
WHY DO YOU HAVE ALL THOSE SWEETS WITH YOU!?
CAN I HAVE SOME TOO?
OKAY, WE'RE HEADING OUT!
PI ピ
PI (BEEP) ピ
Destination: Confirmed
Visibility: Good
Altitude: Confirmed
inates
Propulsion: Launch
PI ピ
PI ピ
FLY... ♪

DOU (VROOM)
YAHOO!
...HIGH! ☆
TOKI-TATSU-SAMA.

IT IS TIME FOR YOU TO JOIN THE ROUND TABLE.
YES...
THANK YOU.

ピ PI (BEEP)
ピ PI
ッ

ZAA (VWAAA)

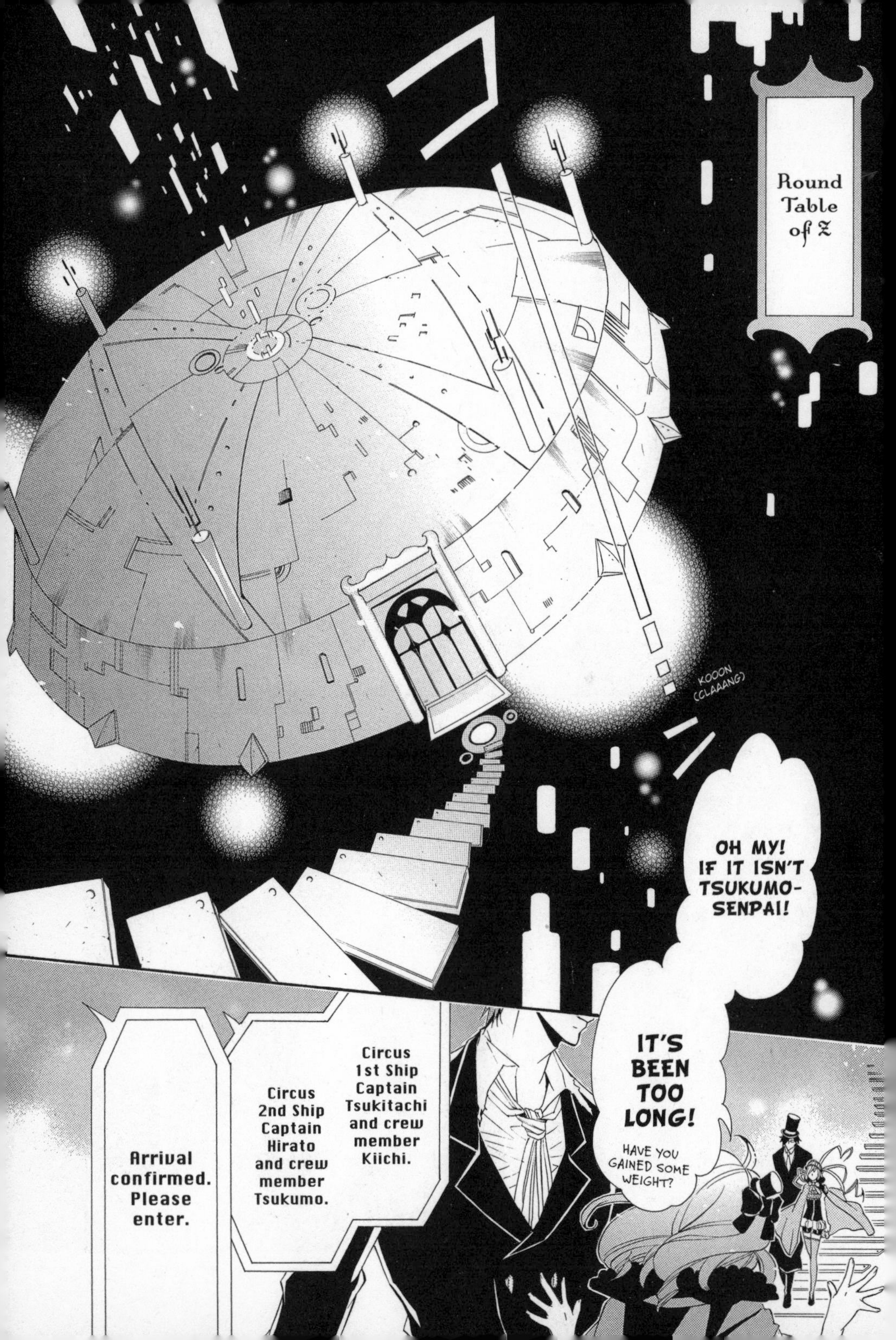
Round Table of Z
KOOON (CLAAANG)
OH MY! IF IT ISN'T TSUKUMO-SENPAI!
IT'S BEEN TOO LONG!
HAVE YOU GAINED SOME WEIGHT?
Circus 1st Ship Captain Tsukitachi and crew member Kiichi.
Circus 2nd Ship Captain Hirato and crew member Tsukumo.
Arrival confirmed. Please enter.

ゴゴ
GOGO (GROOO)
コーーン
KOOON (KAAANG)
コーーン
KOOON

...!
ZAKA (KREESH)
HIDE IN THE SHADOWS!
LET GO ...!
YOU'RE ...
...HERE FOR NAI-CHAN AGAIN?
SU (SWF)
VA-RUGA ...!
BU (BZZ)
BU
BU
THERE'S NO MARGIN FOR ERROR IN A BATTLE...
...SO FIGHTING REALLY DOES SCARE ME.
BUT...
POU (GLOW)

...THERE ARE TIMES...
...WHEN YOU'VE GOT NO CHOICE BUT TO FIGHT.
RE-LEASE!
KIN (CLANG)
PAAAAA (GLEEEAM)
BRIMMING WITH MANLY COMPAS-SION...

GU (GRIP)
THE SHINING PRINCE WITH A SOARING HEART!!
NATIONAL SUPREME DEFENSE FORCE "CIRCUS" ...
...2ND SHIP COMBAT SPECIALIST, YOGI!
KIN

ZAN (STAB)
BUN (VWIP)
THERE SURE ARE...
...A LOT OF THEM!
DAN (BAMF)
GUKU (SWOOP)

NAI-KUN...
Be seated.
First, your reports on "Kafka"...
...the dark organization that opposes us and defiles the living beings of this land.
WE'VE DETERMINED THAT NONE OF THE CORPORATIONS CURRENTLY SUSPECTED OF WORKING WITH KAFKA WILL BE EASILY CAUGHT.
IN FACT, IF WE WERE TO MOVE CLUMSILY, WE BELIEVE THEY ARE PREPARED TO ENTRAP US IN TURN.
IN ADDITION...

THE FORMERLY INSIGNIFICANT NUMBER OF VARUGA SEEMS TO HAVE INCREASED DRASTICALLY.

We have confirmed this from your written report.

Kafka is making copious use of the research they have taken from us.

Research that we had deemed forbidden and sealed away...

The result is the birth of these beings whose physical capabilities far outstrip our own.

Though, as their sentient core seems to be lost in the transition, these beings must be considered degenerations of humankind.

We must endeavor to protect the countless lives endangered by our former colleagues' mistakes.

Now then, Hirato ...

About the boy "Nai" currently being examined in the Research Tower...

Wait.

Will you allow us to ask the questions from here on?
You really are most kind, aren't you...
...Circus Chief Commander Tokitatsu?
I BELIEVE I ALREADY EXPLAINED ...
...THAT IF YOU MOVE, WE WILL NOT RECEIVE ACCURATE DATA!
びくぅ
BIKUU (STARTLE)

I REALIZE YOU WERE RAISED IN A BACKWATER...

...BUT YOU SHOULD AT LEAST KNOW HOW TO BEHAVE DURING A MEDICAL EXAMINATION!

AWA (PANIC) あわ

AWA あわ

HIGHBROW AS ALWAYS, I SEE. AND YOU ONLY JUST TURNED THIRTY-THREE!

WHEN WILL WE HAVE CONCLUSIVE RESULTS? I KNOW THERE'S NO PRECEDENT FOR THIS CASE...
...AND I'M SURE THERE ARE QUITE A LOT OF DATA POINTS YOU'D NEED TO COLLECT, BUT...
WATA (FLUSTER) わたっ
WATA わたっ

INDEED THERE ARE.
BUT PLEASE DON'T FORGET...
FU (HMPH)
...I'M THE ONE ON THE CASE.

IF IT'S WITHIN TECHNOLOGICAL MEANS TO COLLECT THIS DATA, I WILL HAVE IT BY TOMORROW.
I PREFER NOT TO HAVE OUR BOORISH SUPERIORS SPOUTING THEIR DEMANDS AROUND HERE ANYHOW.
PI (BEEP)
PI
GAREKI. ARE YOU OKAY?
I AM WAY PAST THE POINT FOR DUMB QUESTIONS RIGHT NOW.
MAX
IRA (IRRITATED)
IRA
TAKE A LOOK AT THIS.

はっ
PA (POP)
DATA FROM REFLEX TEST A FOR GAREKI, AGE FIFTEEN!
PER TEST RESULTS 1-13, YOU ARE IN PERFECT CONDITION—MINUS YOUR PERSONALITY.

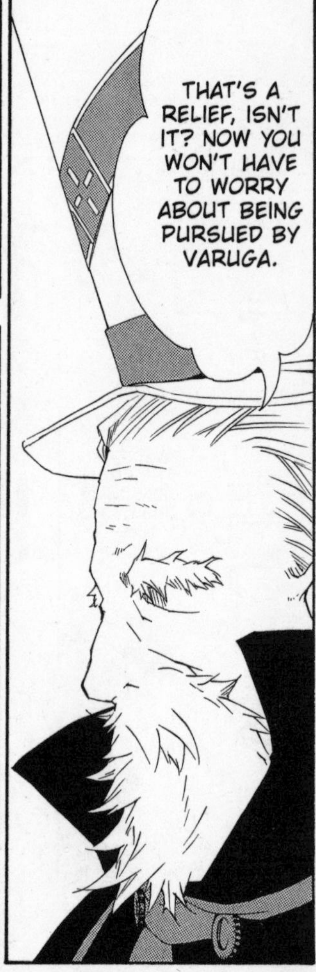

THAT'S A RELIEF, ISN'T IT? NOW YOU WON'T HAVE TO WORRY ABOUT BEING PURSUED BY VARUGA.

IT'S A GOOD THING IT DIDN'T END UP ENTERING YOUR BLOOD...
ENTERING MY BLOOD?

THAT REMINDS ME. WHERE IS THAT YOGI?
NO CLUE.
HE WAS GONE BY THE TIME I WOKE UP.
SOOO (SNEAK)
NO ONE ELSE IS IN THERE, RIGHT?
WHAT ARE YOU DOING?
WAH!

BI (CLICK)
ビッ

OH, IT'S YOU...
UGH!
DOCTOR AKARI...

AND YOU'RE CHANGING YOUR PATCH EVERY DAY AS PRESCRIBED, I TRUST!?
GUKI (TWIST)
UH... Y—
...DON'T TAKE ALLERGIES LIGHTLY, OR YOU'LL LIVE TO REGRET IT.
YES, SIR!

*MEDICINAL PATCH: RELEASES MEDICINE INTO THE BODY WHEN APPLIED

YOU MAY FEEL A LITTLE LIGHT-HEADED DUE TO MINOR ANEMIA.
STAY QUIETLY IN YOUR ROOM FOR NOW.

I APOLOGIZE FOR MY PUPIL.
DR. AKARI IS SO SCARY! I REMEMBER THAT ONE TIME...AND THAT OTHER DAY, HE...
IT SEEMS MY LESSONS ON BEDSIDE MANNER NEVER QUITE MADE IT INTO HIS THICK SKULL...
YOUR ROOMS ARE ON THIS FLOOR.
THE MASTER DOCTOR IS SO WONDER-FUL! ♥

IT'S PITCH-BLACK OUT THERE.
...WHAT DOES?
THAT AREA.
IT LOOKS LIKE THE PLACE I LIVED WITH KAROKU!
THE GEEZER SAID THAT NAI'S TRUE (?) FORM IS THAT OF AN ANIMAL CALLED A "NIJI."
WEST OF MY CITY, WHERE I FIRST MET NAI, I'M PRETTY SURE THERE'S A PLACE CALLED "THE RAINBOW FOREST"...

*NIJI CAN ALSO MEAN "RAINBOW" IN JAPANESE.

I DON'T HAVE ANY INTEREST IN FORESTS...
...AND I HEARD THERE WASN'T ANYTHING ESPECIALLY NOTABLE ABOUT IT ANYWAY.

AND EVER SINCE THAT TIME, I...

...HAD NEVER THOUGHT TO LEAVE THAT CITY.

I THOUGHT IF I STAYED IN A FILTHY PLACE AMONG FILTHY PEOPLE...
...I'D BE ABLE TO HOLD ONTO MY WRATH AGAINST THEM FOREVER.

IT'S OKAY.
I HAVEN'T LOST IT YET.

BUT...

I GET THE FEELING THAT SINCE I MET YOU, I'VE SEEN NOTHING BUT PRETTY SIGHTS.

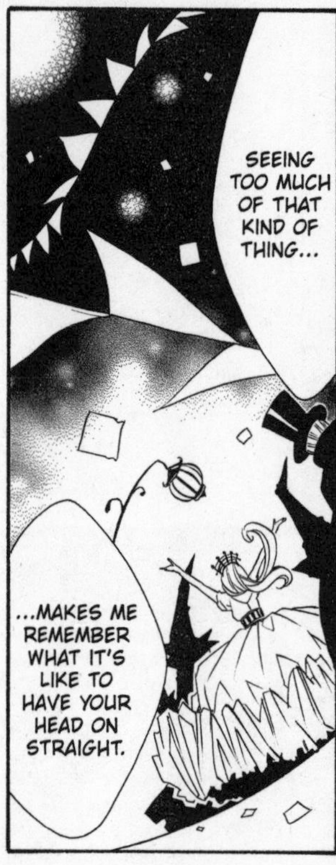
SEEING TOO MUCH OF THAT KIND OF THING...
...MAKES ME REMEMBER WHAT IT'S LIKE TO HAVE YOUR HEAD ON STRAIGHT.

BUT I DON'T WANT TO GROW UP...
...AND FORGET ...

...AND BE THE ONLY ONE TO GO OFF AND LIVE A COMFORTABLE LIFE ON MY OWN.

BUT...

...WHAT IF SUBCONSCIOUSLY, I SECRETLY DID WANT TO LEAVE THERE?

MAYBE I SHOULD GO BACK...

THEN DO PRETTY THINGS LOOK PRETTY...

...IN YOUR EYES TOO, GAREKI?

I ONLY MEANT TO GET NAI AWAY FROM THERE, BUT WHAT IF I WAS GIVING MYSELF A WAY OUT TOO?

YOU'RE TALKING ABOUT ...

...PRETTY THINGS, RIGHT?

KA (FLASH)

BEAM OF PURITY

IF GOING WITH NAI WAS REALLY ME RUNNING AWAY FROM EVERYTHING, I...

?
?
GAREKI?
WHAT'S WRONG?
ARE YOU SLEEPY?
I'M ANEMIC RIGHT NOW.
IT'S OKAY. I STILL HAVE PLENTY OF WRATH.
I'M STILL PLENTY FILTHY.
KOOON
KOOON (KLAAANG)
Akari-kun, give us your report.
Yes, sir.

Please follow along on the copies of the report before you.
The genetic patterns that make up Nai's body...
...bear a resemblance to the genetic makeup of our enemies, the Varuga.
The major point of discrep-ancy is...
...in the Varuga, their mutated cells were derived from their own human cells originally.
Whereas with Nai, his cells are made up of human and niji cells...
...co-existing perfectly in his body.
They are so successfully integrated that Nai can be said to be an entirely new species.
The person that engineered such a union...
...could only be called...

...I suppose.

All data must be recorded.

What?
While it pains me to say it...
...our own technology cannot replicate the genius of this work.
In dissecting the subject...
...who can say how much invaluable data we would unwittingly lose?

And as a researcher myself, I feel...

...the successful realization of a creation as perfect as Nai...

...would make him very precious to the one who created him as well.

As such...

......

......Very well.
In that case...
...I shall revise my orders.

FU (SIGH)
PU (BOOP)
HIRATO ANTICI-PATED THIS...
...AND SPOKE TO YOU BEFOREHAND, DIDN'T HE?
HE COULD SEE THE DIRECTION THEY WERE HEADING, HM?

PLEASE DON'T GET ME WRONG.
I CERTAINLY DIDN'T DO THIS TO PLEASE THAT UPSTART.
PLEASE DON'T EVEN JOKE ABOUT THAT...

WE WERE SIMPLY OF THE SAME OPINION THIS TIME.
AND IT CERTAINLY DOESN'T HURT TO DEMONSTRATE EVERY NOW AND THEN JUST HOW MUCH TRUST THE HIGHER-UPS PLACE IN ME.

THE RAINBOW FOREST?

THAT'S RIGHT.

IT SEEMS TO BE THE PLACE YOU AND KAROKU LIVED TOGETHER.

YOUR ORIGINS ARE MUCH MORE COMPLEX THAN I HAD IMAGINED.

THOSE ORIGINS...

...WILL LIKELY CONTINUE TO CAUSE YOU A GOOD DEAL OF TROUBLE GOING FORWARD.

THE GOVERN-MENT—US INCLUDED...
...AND MANY OTHERS WHO WILL WANT TO USE YOU WILL CONTINUALLY PURSUE YOU.
HOWEVER...

NO MATTER WHAT THE CIRCUMSTANCES ...
...REMEMBER THAT YOUR TIME ON THIS EARTH BELONGS ONLY TO YOU.

YOU SHOULD DECIDE FOR YOURSELF WHAT IT IS YOU WANT TO DO.
AND THOUGH I CAN'T PROMISE ANYTHING AFTERWARD ...

...IF YOU DECIDE YOU DON'T WANT TO WORK WITH US AND WANT TO LEAVE HERE...
...I'LL BE SURE TO BE VERY SOUND ASLEEP TONIGHT.

...!

I...
...WANT TO GO...
...TO THE RAINBOW FOREST.
I WANT TO BECOME ABLE...
...TO FULLY UNDER-STAND THE THINGS KAROKU SAID.
ALSO, I...
IF WE GO TO KAROKU'S HOUSE...
...WE'LL LEARN EVEN MORE THINGS, RIGHT?

...WANT TO LEARN LOTS OF THINGS...
...AND THINK ABOUT LOTS OF THINGS.

I WANT TO BE ABLE TO UNDER-STAND...
...THE THINGS ALL OF YOU ARE THINKING BETTER TOO.

THEN...
...OUR VECTORS NOW SHALL CROSS.
SO THAT WE MAY FIND...
...THE PIECE THAT WILL CONNECT THE PAST TO THE FUTURE.

TO THE RAINBOW FOREST!

KARNEVAL

KARNEVAL

Score 10: The Rainbow Forest

THE RAINBOW FOREST? IT'S A RATHER DANGEROUS SPOT, ISN'T IT?
IF YOU WERE TO BE INJURED OUT THERE, DR. AKARI, JUST THINK HOW THE LADIES WOULD GRIEVE AROUND HERE!
YOU'RE QUITE POPULAR, YOU KNOW?

WELL, WHEN IT COMES TO LADIES...
...I'M AFRAID I DON'T CARE ENOUGH TO BE BOTHERED...

PLEASE END UP STRANDED IN THE WOODS FOR HALF A YEAR OR SOMETHING.
JUST BECAUSE HE'S GOT LOOKS, MONEY, AND STATUS DOESN'T MEAN WOMEN WILL JUST FALL AT HIS FEET, YOU KNOW!
DANG IT ALL!
PLEASE COME ORDER FROM US AGAIN, DR. AKARI!
IF ONLY SOMEONE WOULD REJECT THAT MAN HORRIBLY!
DOCTOR!
WE REALLY APPRECIATE ALL THE SWEETS! ♥
I LOVE YOU, DOCTOR!
JUST SEEING YOU ALL HAPPY MAKES ME HAPPY.

LAB TECHS? ARE THEY COMING TOO?
YEP, YEP!
THEY'RE RESEARCHERS FROM THE RESEARCH TOWER.
DONYORI (GLOOOOM)
......
WHAT?
SUKU (RISE)
D-
DR. AKARI IS RIDING WITH US!!
RIGHT BESIDE ME, IN FACT!!

ONCE, HE REFUSED TO GIVE ME ANESTHETICS, YELLED AT ME, AND SHOVED A TOWEL IN MY MOUTH, AND...
...AND HE FORCED ME TO DRINK THAT AWFUL-TASTING MEDICINE OVER AND OVER—
HE HAD ME TIED DOWN TOO...
OPERATION TRAUMA, HUH?
LET'S GET ON BOARD.

UM...
ARE YOU OKAY?

NAI-CHAN!
WAAAH! WAAAH!
I'LL TRY REALLY HARD!

UM...
DESTINATION...
...SET FOR THE RAINBOW FOREST...
PI (BEEP) PI

NOW...
...LATCHING!

TO WHAT?
UH!
LAUNCH...
LAUNCHING...
...I MEAN...
BUUN (VROOO)
PAAAA (FWAAAH)

KACHA (RATTLE)
ALL OF YOU, TAKE THESE.
WHAT ARE THEY?
SOUND MARKERS.
AS WE MOVE THROUGH THE FOREST, WE'LL USE THESE TO MARK OUR PATH BACK.

THE ENVIRONS OF THE RAINBOW FOREST ARE HIGHLY UNUSUAL.
THE PLANT LIFE OF THIS AREA HAS DEVELOPED A CELLULAR MAKEUP THAT INCORPORATES LIGHT-REFLECTING PROPERTIES.
SINCE THIS FOREST IS BORDERED ON ALL SIDES BY THE OCEAN, THERE IS A LARGE AMOUNT OF WATER MOLECULES IN THE AIR.
BETWEEN THAT AND THE LIGHT-REFLECTING PROPERTIES OF THE LOCAL FLORA, THERE IS QUITE A BIT OF LIGHT REFRACTION IN THE AIR...
...RESULTING IN A LARGE NUMBER OF RAINBOWS IN THE SKIES OVERHEAD.
IT IS FROM THIS THAT THE FOREST DERIVES ITS NAME.
KON (KNOCK)
BUT IT ISN'T ONLY IN THE SKY...
...THAT THIS PHENOMENON OCCURS.

THE REFRACTION IS KNOWN TO CREATE MIRAGES ON THE GROUND AS WELL.
IN SOME CASES, THE LANDSCAPE WE OBSERVE ...
...MAY VERY WELL BE *ENTIRELY DIFFERENT* FROM WHAT'S ACTUALLY THERE.
AS SUCH, IT IS VERY COMMON TO LOSE ONE'S WAY IN THIS FOREST.
WHAT'S MORE, DUE TO SOME FORM OF SEISMIC WAVE IN THE AREA, COMMUNICATION DEVICES ARE ALSO KNOWN TO MALFUNC-TION.
check.
THUS...
...THE MOST RELIABLE MEANS OF FINDING ONE'S WAY IN THIS FOREST IS...

...THROUGH SOUND.
SO THAT'S IT.
IF NAI USED TO BE ONE OF THOSE ANIMALS THAT LIVE HERE...
...THAT EXPLAINS WHY HIS SENSE OF HEARING IS SO GOOD.
WHAT ARE YOU DOING?
GURA (JIGGLE)
グラ
グラ
GURA
ARE YOU A CHILD ...?
YES, OF COURSE YOU ARE.
キュイン
KYUIN (PEWT)
KYUIN
キュイン
NO...
I'M AN ADULT ...

LUNCH BOXES ...?
THEY FORGOT TO PACK THESE THIS MORNING.
AND THEY WON'T BE ABLE TO FIND TRUST-WORTHY FOODSTUFFS IN THE FOREST.

NAI'S (FOR-MER) DIET ...

MUSSHO (MUNCH)

MUSSHO

...CON-SISTED OF IN-SECTS.

IT SEEMS.

GUUUU (GRUMBLE)

IF HE GETS HUNGRY IN THE FOREST, WOULD HE...?

PASHII (SNATCH)

FOREST FOOD-STUFFS

......

I'LL GO...

...IMME-DIATELY!

FOOD FOR THE ENTIRE PARTY

THANK YOU!

PIII (TWEE)
PIII
CHI (CHIRP)
CHI
CHI
GASA (RUSTLE)

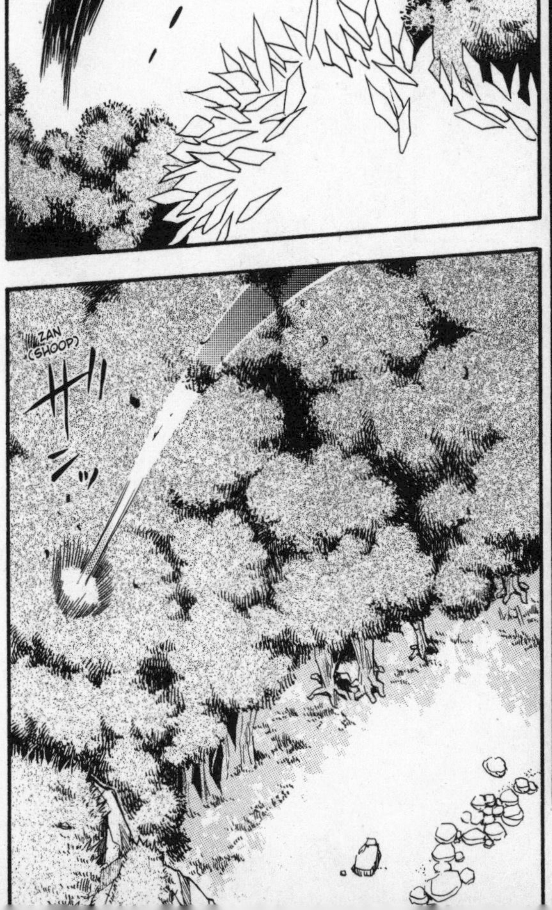
ZAA (ZHAAAM)
ZAN (SHOOP)

The Rainbow Forest
AH!

たたたっ
TA (THP)
TA
TA
がしいっ
GASHII (GRASP)
TODAY ...
...YOU DO NOT LET GO OF MY HAND, UNDER-STAND?
THIS DUMMY'S WANDERED OFF ON HIS OWN THREE TIMES NOW.
I DEFINITELY CAN'T AFFORD TO LET HIM GET LOST IN A PLACE LIKE THIS!
?
?

NOW THEN, WE WILL BEGIN MAKING OUR WAY TOWARD OUR GOAL, "KAROKU'S HOUSE."
AS IT STANDS, WE HAVE ONLY NAI'S SENSES AND MEMORY OF THE PLACE TO GUIDE US TO OUR DESTINATION.
BUT WE WILL USE THE SOUND MARKERS TO LAY DOWN A SOLID RETURN PATH.
SO BE SURE TO MARK OUR TRAIL OFTEN AND WELL!
MINE IS GAREKI-KUN!
AS WE MOVE FORWARD...
...BE SURE TO KEEP TRACK OF YOUR ASSIGNED PARTNER'S PRESENCE AT ALL TIMES.
EVERYONE HAS BEEN SPRAYED WITH INSECT REPELLANT, I TRUST?
DON'T COME CRYING TO ME IF SOMETHING BURROWS INTO YOUR SKIN.
DONE!
DONE!

AS THIS IS A HIGHLY UNUSUAL FOREST...
...THERE ARE SURE TO BE ANY NUMBER OF SCIENTIFICALLY NOTEWORTHY SIGHTS ALONG THE WAY.
AND THOUGH I'M SURE THE TEMPTATION TO STOP AND COLLECT SAMPLES WILL BE POWERFUL...
...DO NOT STOP FOR ANY REASON DURING OUR HIKE WITHOUT ALERTING ME FIRST.
QUES-TIONS?
NO, SIR!
THEN LET'S MOVE OUT!
ASSIGNED TO MONITOR

ザカ
ZAKA (RUSTLE)
ザカ
ZAKA

IT'S BEEN ABOUT AN HOUR.
HE'S BEEN LEADING US THROUGH THIS UNDEFINED TERRAIN UNWAVERINGLY THE WHOLE TIME.

THIS WAY.

WAIT.

YOU DON'T MEAN WE NEED TO SCALE THIS ROCK, DO YOU?

SU (SWOOF)

!
A MIRAGE ...!?

SAA (FWOOH)
WE HAVE TOO LITTLE INTEL ON THIS AREA...
WHAT A BEAUTIFUL PLACE!
WHAT IS THIS PLACE ...?
IT DIDN'T SHOW UP ON ANY AERIAL RECON-NAISSANCE PHOTOS OF THE FOREST ...
KAROKU'S HOUSE IS JUST OVER THERE!
ZA (RUSTLE)

NOTHING'S BURNED EXCEPT THE HOUSE.
THIS WASN'T CAUSED BY A FOREST FIRE. SEARCH FOR CLUES!

IF WE HADN'T HAD HIM...
...REGULAR HUMANS LIKE OURSELVES COULD NEVER HAVE FOUND THIS PLACE.

MEANING WHOEVER CAME TO ERASE THIS EVIDENCE...
...WASN'T HUMAN.

IT HASN'T BEEN MORE THAN A FEW DAYS.
SEARCH FOR ANY UNBURNT FRAG-MENTS THAT REMAIN!
GARA (CLATTER)

WE CAN STILL TAKE THEM BACK TO THE LAB FOR ANALYSIS! THIS IS WHERE YOU PROVE WHAT YOU'RE MADE OF!
YES, SIR!

CHEER UP, NAI-CHAN.
EVEN IF THE HOUSE BURNED DOWN...
THERE'S ALSO THE PLACE THAT I STAYED.

WHERE?
LET'S GO!

A CAVE?
HA (GASP)
GO (SWOOP)
BASHI (SLASH)

ビキ
BIKI (WRITHE)
ビキッ
BIKI
DORN KISTE!!
ZAN (SLICE)

ボト
BOTO (PLOP)
ドッ
DO (THUD)
ドッ
DO
ボト
BOTO
ドッ
DO
ドッ
DO
ドシャ
DOSHA (SLAM)
チ
CHI (CHEEP)
チィ
CHII
チィ
CHII
STAY PUT.
!
...!
チィ
CHII
チ
CHI
チィ
CHII
バシィ
BASHII (WHAP)
ドシャ
DOSHA (SLAM)
DID...
DID I DO IT...?
ハァ
HAA (PANT)
ハ
HA
ばっ
BA (DASH)
NAI!?

STOP ...!!

GA (TRIP)

!?

TAKE COVER!

ZAN (FOOSH)

ZAAA (SWOOP)

THERE'S STILL MORE OF THEM...!!

BUCHI (YANK)

THEY'RE AFTER NAI!
YOGI!!

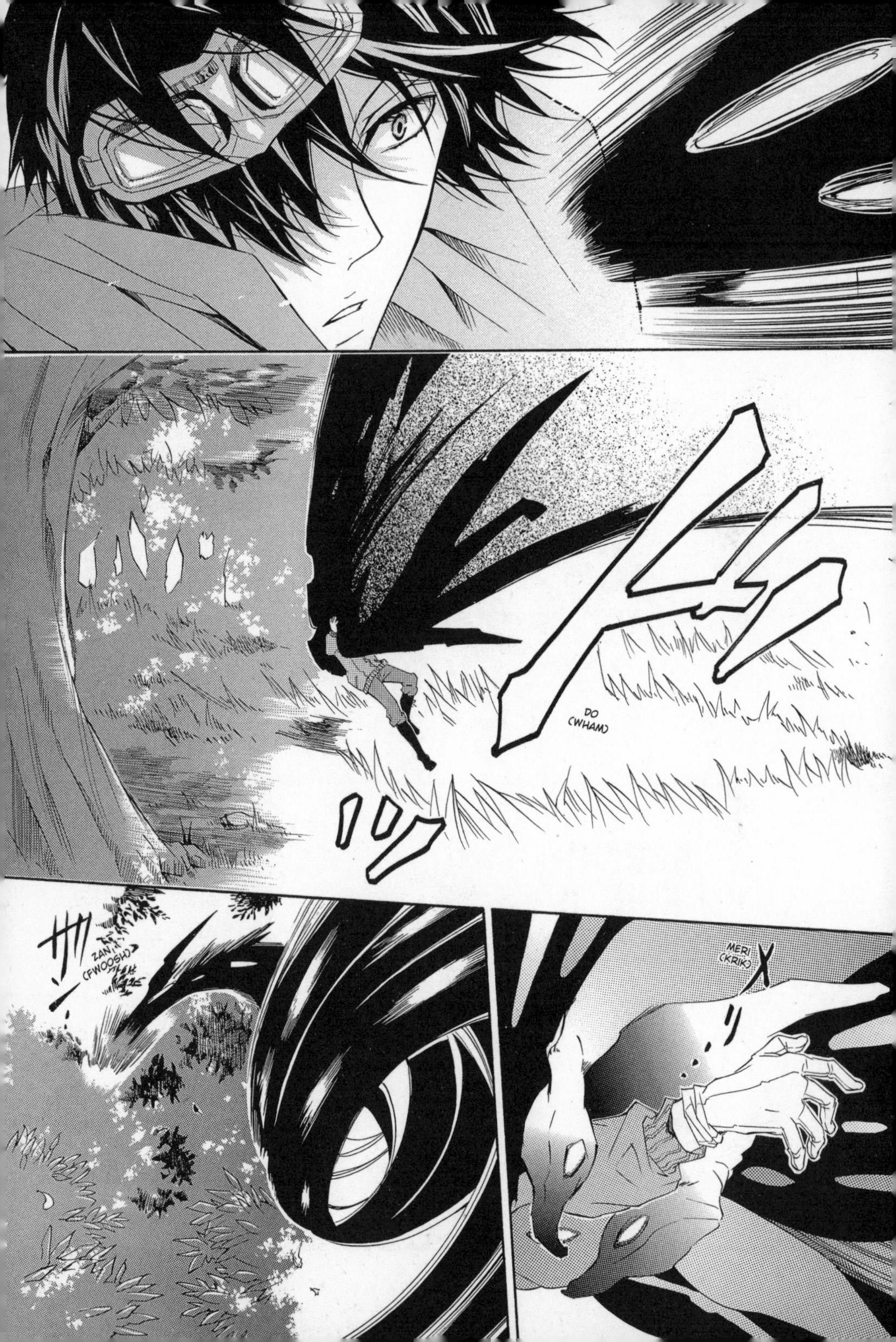

DO (WHAM)
ZAN (FWOOSH)
MERI (KRIK)

GA—

THEY WERE AFTER GAREKI-KUN ...!?

GAREKI-KUN...!!

Score 11: Eva

GAREKI-KUN...!!
DR. AKARI!
TAKE NAI-CHAN ...!

ZAN (VWOOSH)

HE'S FINE...!

YOU HAVE TO BELIEVE HE'S FINE ...!!

はっ

HA (GASP)

ZAN (ZHAP)
ZA (ZHAK)
ZA
ZA
ZA
DAN (WHOOMP)
BA (WHIP)

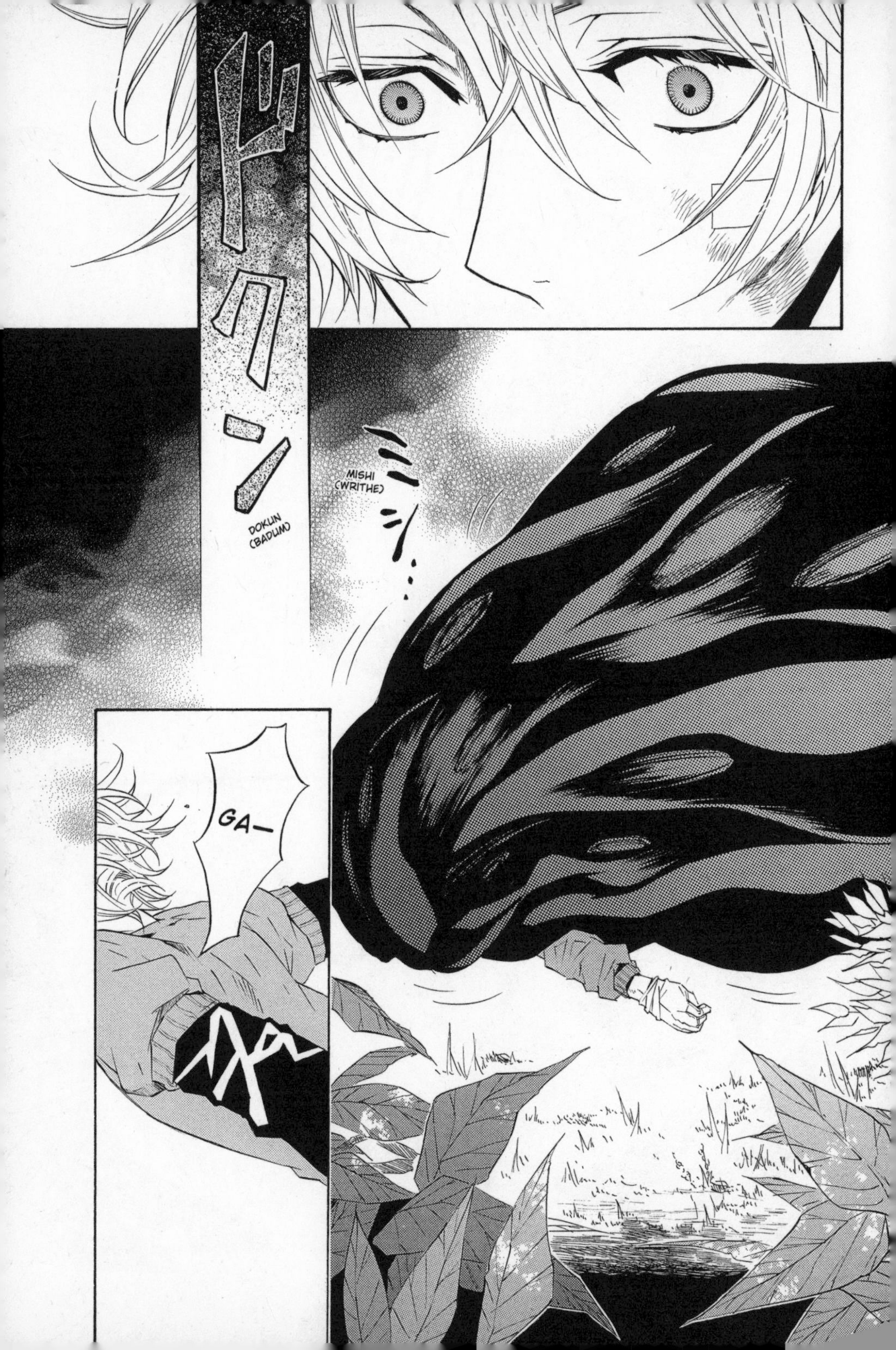
DOKUN
(BADUM)
MISHI
(WRITHE)
GA—

KRONE SAPHIR.
DO (VWOOM)

THE GEMS OBEY MY WORD...
...AND BURY EVIL IN THE BRILLIANCE OF THEIR SPARKLE.
I TAKE THE NAME OF QUEEN OF THE JEWELED CROWN!

BARA (SPLATTER)
BARA
NATIONAL SUPREME DEFENSE FORCE "CIRCUS"...
...2ND SHIP COMBAT SPECIALIST, EVA!
THOSE WHO DO NOT ACCEPT MY LOVE...
...CAN SHATTER TO DUST!!

EVA-NEE-SAN!!
WHAT ARE YOU DOING HE—
SHUN (FLAP)
SHUN
WHY YOU...
...DIM-WIT!!
GO (THWAK)
DUNCE!
GO
YOU'D BETTER BE GRATEFUL TO ME!!
GO
FUWA (WAFT)...
YOGI'S MOOD
CAN YOU MOVE, BOY?
GU (PUSH)
GAREKI-KUN!!
GABA (JUMP)

AH!
AH!
DON'T STRAIN YOUR-SELF!!
DOES IT HURT REALLY BAD ANY-WHERE!?
...
DO YOU FEEL STRANGE OR SICK AT ALL!?
...
じわ
JIWA (TEARS)
I'M SORRY ...
YOU'RE SO SCARED YOU CAN'T EVEN SPEAK, CAN YOU...!!?
IF ONLY I'D BEEN FASTER...
ぎゅっ
GYUU (HUG)
...
THAT'S NOT IT!!
I JUST NEEDED A MOMENT TO PROCESS EVERY-THING, OKAY!?
LET GO!!

SERIOUSLY—
BUT NEE-SAN...
...WHAT ARE YOU DOING OUT HERE?
WELL, I WAS IN GAVAN CHASING THAT
GEEZER
AROUND TOWN...
AND THEN THE WRETCH MANAGED TO ESCAPE FROM ME...
TCH!
SO TO RELIEVE MY IRE, I THOUGHT I'D GO GAZE UPON MY DARLING♥ TSUKUMO'S FACE.
PERA (BLAB)
I HEARD SHE'D COME HERE TO THE RAINBOW FOREST, SO I CAME TOO BUT GOT HERE AHEAD OF HER, I GUESS.
PERA
HUH? TSUKUMO-CHAN'S COMING TOO?
GAZING UPON MEN'S FACES DOESN'T GIVE ME ANY SOLACE AT ALL.
ONLY BEINGS OF CUTENESS WILL DO!
I WAS FOLLOWING YOUR TRAIL OF SOUND MARKERS...
...WHEN I SAW THE VARUGA AND RAN IN TO JOIN THE BATTLE. BUT NOW I HAVE NO IDEA WHERE WE ARE.
WHERE ARE WE?
I CAN'T HEAR THE SOUND MARKERS AT ALL ANYMORE.
UM...
I KIND OF PLUNGED INTO THE FOREST CHASING AFTER GAREKI-KUN TOO...
SO...
HUH?
YOU MEAN... WE'RE LOST!?

THEY'LL BE FINE.
THEIR INJURIES ARE EQUIVALENT TO A BRUISE ON A HUMAN.
THAT SAID, LEAVING THEM IN THIS WEAKENED STATE OUT IN THE WILD...
...IS TANTAMOUNT TO A DEATH SENTENCE.
I'LL TAKE THEM.
GAREKI AND YOGI...
...ARE THEY OKAY?
THIS HAPPENED BECAUSE I MOVED WHEN I WASN'T SUPPOSED TO, DIDN'T IT...?

THAT'S PRECISELY RIGHT. HOWEVER...
...MAKE NO MISTAKE AS TO THE ACTUAL CAUSE OF THIS.
FUU (SIGH)

THOSE WHO ATTACKED US ARE THE ONES TRULY TO BLAME.

BUT THEY CERTAINLY ARE TAKING A WHILE...
THIS IS BAD.

MY ASSISTANTS WHO REMAINED BEHIND AT THE BURNED-OUT HOUSE SHOULD BE ALL RIGHT.
THEY SHOULD KNOW WHAT TO DO IN CASE OF EMERGENCY.
—TOR! DOCTOR!

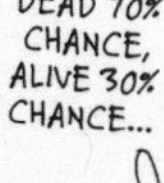
IN THIS SITUATION, CHANCES ARE HIGH THAT THEY WERE KILLED.
DEAD 70% CHANCE, ALIVE 30% CHANCE...

GASA (RUSTLE)
DOC—

DOC-TOR!!
I'M SO SORRY I DISLIKED YOU BEFORE!
I MISSED YOU SO MUCH!
I THOUGHT WE WERE GOING TO BE LOST IN THE WILD FOREVER!
OH REALLY?
YOU DISLIKED ME, HM?
WAAAH!
...
WHAT HAP-PENED?
GAREKI GOT HURT!?
HE WAS UNSTEADY ON HIS FEET.
AND WE COULDN'T HAVE HIM WOBBLING AROUND WHILE WE SEARCHED FOR YOU, COULD WE?
I THREATENED TO KISS HIM IF HE STRUGGLED.
WHY, EVA...?
SOME-ONE KILL ME NOW.
I THINK GAREKI-KUN WOULD'VE PREFERRED IT IF I CARRIED HIM PIGGYBACK...

YOU DON'T SEEM TO HAVE ANY SERIOUS INJURIES, BUT YOU NEED TO TAKE IT EASY.
GO BACK TO THE SHIP AT THE FOREST'S ENTRANCE WITH EVA.
EVA.
TAKE HIM, PLEASE.
CERTAINLY. ♥
GAREKI ...!
I'M... SORRY!
HUH?
FOR WHAT?

NOW THEN ...
...BACK TO OUR ORIGINAL OBJECTIVE BEFORE THAT LITTLE INTERRUPTION.
CHI (TWEE) チ
CHI チ
CHI チ
CHI チ
CHI チ

HERE'S HOPING SOMETHING OF YOUR LIFE HERE WITH KAROKU REMAINS.

KA...
...ROKU
...
?
ごしっ
GOSHI
(RUB)
THIS
IS...

...THE PLACE THAT NAI-CHAN...
...LIVED WITH HIM...
EVERYTHING SEEMS TO HAVE BEEN CAREFULLY CRAFTED.
I APOLOGIZE, BUT WE DO NEED TO TAKE IT APART.
YOGI.
PULL EVERYTHING OUT HERE, FOR NOW!
AH! YES, SIR!

"HEY, NAI?
"COME HERE. LOOK AT THIS.
"DO YOU UNDER-STAND?"
YES.
"GOOD."
KAROKU IS WARM.

WARM...
KATA (WHIR)
カタ
KATA
カタ
KATA
カタ
KATA
カタ...

KAROKU-SAMA.

PLEASE GET READY.

IF THIS LIGHT COULD MELT ME...

...I COULD WEEP...

COM-ING.

...FOR THIS WARMTH...

HOW COULD YOU FAIL!?
IT'S AN EASY THING TO COMMAND BUT NOT SO EASY A TASK.
NOT WITH CIRCUS BESIDE HIM.
KAROKU'S INTERESTED IN THAT GAREKI BOY, YOU UNDER-STAND!?
I WANTED TO SURPRISE HIM BY BRINGING GAREKI TO HIM!!
THIS IS A RATHER BIG THING TO DO BEHIND THE CEO'S BACK.
ISN'T THERE SOME OTHER PRESENT YOU COULD GIVE KAROKU-SAMA?
NO MATTER WHAT I GIVE HIM, HIS EXPRESSION NEVER CHANGES.
I WANT HIM TO LIKE ME MORE!

HE IS ALREADY VERY FOND OF YOU.
YOU ARE FOURTEEN YEARS OLD, ELISKA-SAMA.
AND KAROKU-SAMA IS EIGHTEEN.
AGE-WISE, YOU ARE ALREADY WELL SUITED FOR EACH OTHER.
YOU DON'T UNDER-STAND!

I WANT ...
I WANT HIM TO LOVE ME SO MUCH HE WOULD PURSUE ME WITH SUCH FORCE THAT I'D HATE IT!
I WANT HIM TO BE CRAZY ABOUT ME...I WANT HIM TO WANT ME!!

TELL ME!
HOW CAN I MAKE HIM WANT ME!?
WELL ...
THAT'S DIFFICULT FOR ME TO SAY...

HEY!
YOU SHOULD SHOW MORE ENJOYMENT EATING THAT FOOD, DOCTOR!
TSUKUMO WENT TO THE TROUBLE OF BRINGING IT ALL THIS WAY FOR YOU!!
HURRY UP AND EAT.
OUR ERRAND HERE IS FINISHED. WE'RE WASTING TIME THAT COULD BE SPENT IN THE LAB.
WHA!?

TSUKUMO! ♥ I APPRECIATE YOU!
AHH, SOLACE...!
I'M SORRY. IF I'D ONLY ARRIVED SOONER...
E...
EVA...

GAREKI ...
DO YOUR HURT PLACES STILL SMART?
NOTHING HURTS.

...
DID YOU FIND ANYTHING?
EH?

UMM ...
WE DID FIND A NOTEBOOK.
I TOOK A PEEK INSIDE, BUT...

IT WAS FULL OF NUMBERS AND SYMBOLS.
...I COULDN'T REALLY UNDERSTAND IT.
......
I, UH...
SORRY...
I'M HOPELESS AT DECI-PHERING STUFF...
EH HEH...
BUT DR. AKARI WAS REALLY INTERESTED IN IT.
EVERYONE DONE WITH THEIR MEAL START PREPPING FOR OUR RETURN.
WE'RE HEADING BACK NOW!

DON (THUMP)
ド、ン…
DODON
ドドン…
Karasuna, the Illuminated City
The Village of Hami
AH…
フラ…
FURA (WOBBLE)
ズシャ…
ZUSHA (WHUMP)
GA… REKI…

WHAT DO I DO...?
HELP ME, GAREKI...

Score 12: In Karasuna

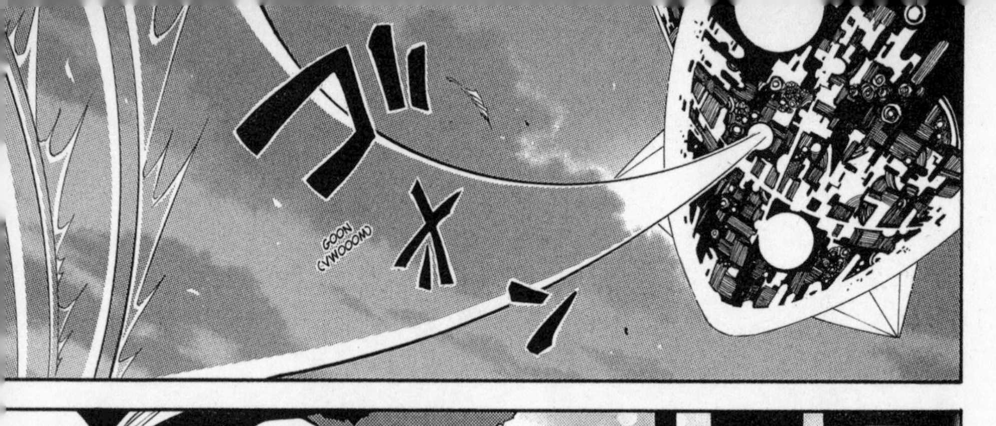
GOON
(VWOOOM)

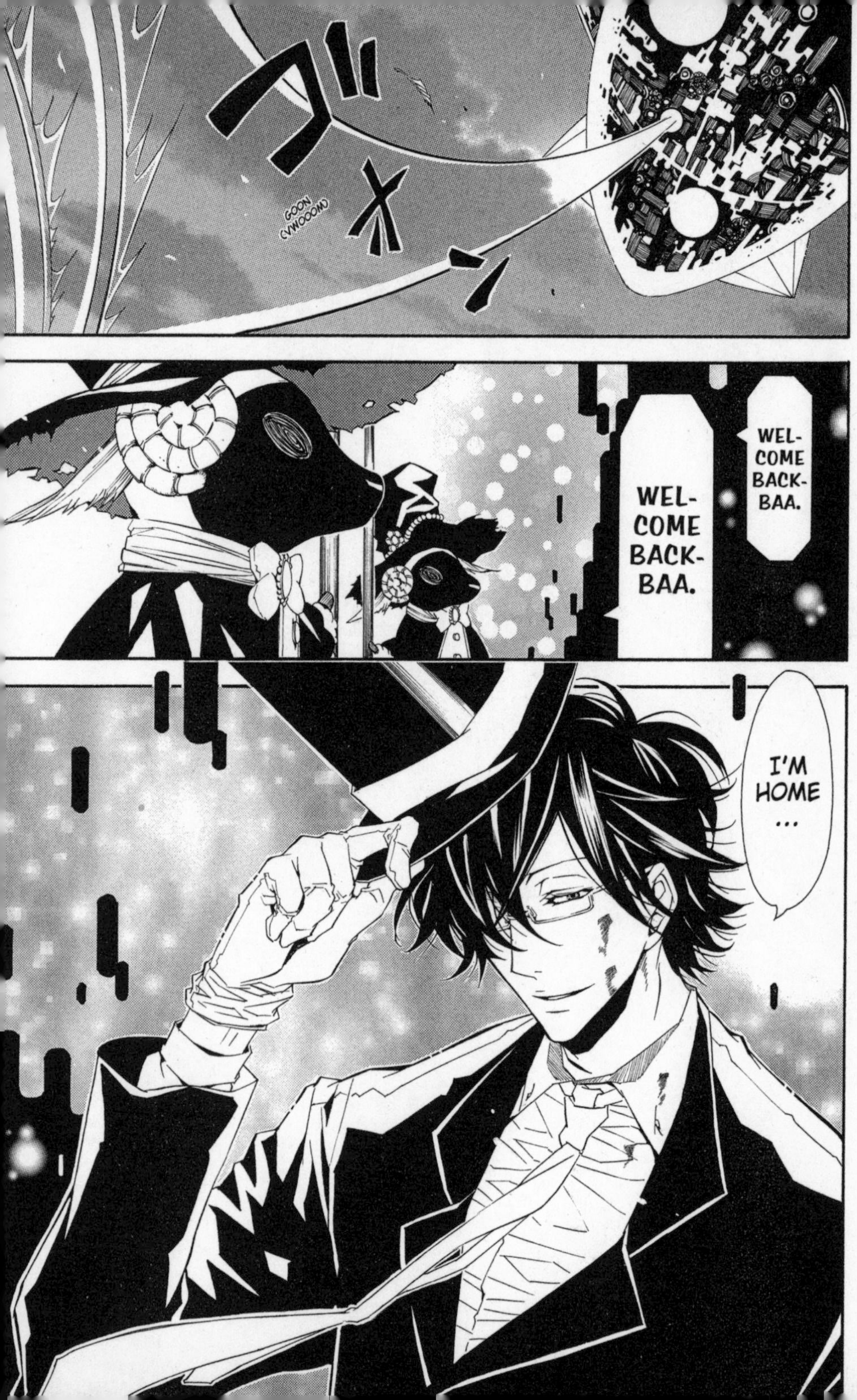

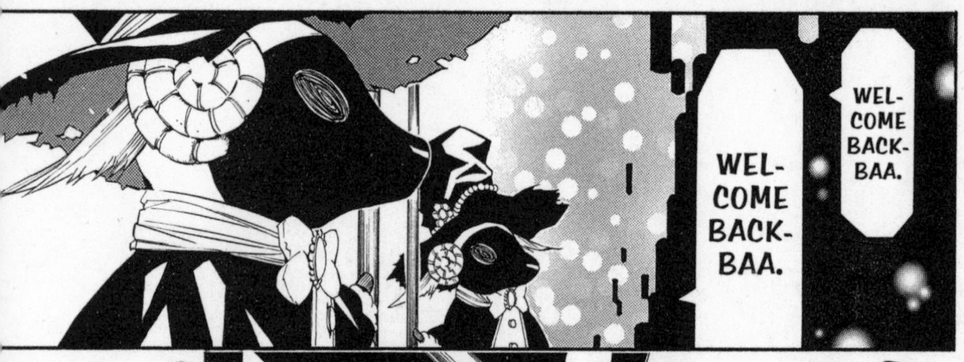
WEL-
COME
BACK-
BAA.
WEL-
COME
BACK-
BAA.

I'M
HOME
...

PIRORIRON (RINGALING)
PIRORIRON
YOGI?
WHAT IS IT?
WELCOME BACK, HIRATO-SAN! ♥
UM, WE'RE JUST ABOUT TO HEAD BACK FROM THE RAINBOW FOREST NOW.
I TOLD YOU!
YOU DON'T NEED TO COME WITH ME!!
NO! NO! I WANT TO GO! I WANT TO GO!

PI (BEEP) ピッ

TOOJI

KARASUNA

THE RAINBOW FOREST

IT LOOKS LIKE IT'S REALLY CLOSE BY.

IT'S THE CITY GAREKI-KUN'S FROM, KARASUNA.

SO...

...HE SAID THERE WAS A PLACE HE WANTED TO STOP THERE...

YOU...

IRA (IRK) イラ IRA イラ

...LET GO OF ME RIGHT NOW.

NO! NO!

...Is that okay?
If possible, Nai-chan wants to go too...
I promise I'll watch over both of them really carefully!
...Is that... a no?

WHAT!?

NO WAY! HE AGREED!?

YEAH.

THAT'S WAY TOO NICE FOR HIM! ICK!!

DIDN'T I REPORT THAT THEY WERE ATTACKED BY VARUGA IN THE FOREST!?

What if it happens again!?

IS THAT EVA?

THAT'S WHY I'M SENDING YOGI.

SOON, THEY WON'T HAVE MUCH OPPORTUNITY TO GO ANYWHERE, SO I'M LETTING THEM GO NOW.

What ...!?

EVA AND TSUKUMO, YOU ARE TO ESCORT THE RESEARCH TEAM BACK TO THE RESEARCH TOWER.

AKARI-SAN'S WITH YOU, ISN'T HE? PUT HIM ON.

HIRATO-SAN SAYS HE'D LIKE TO THANK YOU PERSONALLY FOR A NUMBER OF THINGS.
HERE HE IS!
NO NEED.
HANG UP.
IT'S A WASTE OF BATTERY.

...
HE HEARD THAT.
EH!?
"YOU'RE A GROWN MAN...
"...AND YET YOU EXPRESS YOUR FEELINGS OF LIKE AND DISLIKE FOR OTHERS SO HONESTLY ...
HUH?

"HOW UTTERLY ADORABLE YOU ARE" ...!?
WHAAAT?
YOU WANT ME TO REPEAT THAT WORD-FOR-WORD TO HIM!?
NO WAY!
IF YOU'RE GOING TO PICK A FIGHT, PLEASE DO IT ON YOUR OWN!
WHY DO YOU DISLIKE EACH OTHER SO MUCH!?
I THINK THE DOCTOR GOT THE MESSAGE ALREADY ...
ER, I'LL TAKE THIS INTO THE SHIP, SHALL I?

ISN'T THAT GREAT, NAI-CHAN?
HIRATO-SAN SAID YOU CAN COME ALONG!

PAA (GLEAM)
HE'LL ONLY GET IN THE WAY.
JUST MAKE HIM GO BACK WITH THE RESEARCH TEAM!

BUT NAI-CHAN'S PROBABLY AFRAID TO BE APART FROM YOU.
HUH !?
JUST THINK...
HE'S EXPERIENCED KAROKU-SAN SUDDENLY DISAPPEARING WITHOUT A TRACE, SO...
COME ON!

....
DON'T LEAVE ME HERE!
DON'T LEAVE ME HERE!
OPTICAL MALFUNCTION

OH, FINE, THEN.
YAAAAY!
DAMN.

THIS IS AS FAR AS WE CAN TAKE YOU.

WELL...
TAKE CARE.

BAN (FOOM)

PAAN (FWOOF)
THANK YOU, TSUKUMO-CHAN!

DON (THUMP)
Karasuna, the Illuminated City
DODON
YA KNOW...
I FEEL LIKE IT'S BEEN A LONG TIME SINCE I GOT TO WALK AROUND A TOWN FOR FUN LIKE THIS!
I'M GETTING ALL EXCITED NOW!
KEEP GAPING LIKE AN IDIOT, AND YOU'LL GET PICK-POCKETED.
AH!

PAN
PAN (BANG)
JUST LIKE GAREKI!

OOH!
I WANT THAT LEATHER BRACE-LET!
CAN I GIVE IT A GO!?
HEY ...

PAN
SUKA (CLACK)

PAN
SUKA
PAN
SUKA

YOU'RE PATHETIC. MOVE OVER.
AWW ...
PASHI (SNATCH)

PAN
WOW!
TH—
THANK YOU!
HE NAILED ALL THE PRIZES.
YOU'RE SO COOL, GAREKI-KUN...
YOU MUST BE REALLY POPULAR WITH GIRLS, HUH? LOOKING AT YOU, I FEEL EMBARRASSED...
I BET YOU'VE ALREADY HAD TWO OR THREE GIRL-FRIENDS...
...RIGHT?
GAREKI!!

HUH?
TSUBAME ...?
THANK GOODNESS!
I FINALLY FOUND YOU...
HUH!?
THAT WAS FAST!
GIRLFRIEND A!?
...NO—
HUH!?
YOU'VE GOT IT WRONG!!

I LIKE SLIGHTLY PUDGY BOYS WITH GENTLE EYES!
IT'S MY DREAM TO MARRY ONE!!
GOOOOO (RUMMMBLE)
KAAAAA (BLUUUSH)
I SHOUTED THAT OUT LOUD... I'M SO EMBARRASSED...
THAT...
UM...
...IS THE COMPLETE OPPOSITE OF HIM.
SO?
BIKU (FLINCH)
YOU SAID YOU WERE LOOKING FOR ME?
DID SOMETHING HAPPEN?
I...
I...
I...

I KILLED SOME-ONE...
I DON'T KNOW WHAT TO DO...!
I'M SORRY IT WAS SUCH A LONG WALK.
AND I APOLOGIZE FOR DRAGGING YOUR POOR FRIENDS OUT HERE TOO.
IT WASN'T THAT LONG A WALK.
I HADN'T REALIZED YOU'D MOVED...
...SO THAT'S WHY I COULD NEVER CATCH YOU THERE, NO MATTER HOW OFTEN I WENT.
RIGHT...
WELL, I DIDN'T EXACTLY "MOVE"...

IT'S BEEN ABOUT TWO YEARS SINCE WE LAST TALKED, HUH?
WHERE'S YOUR BROTHER?
YOTAKA'S STILL AT WORK.
I HAD THE EARLY SHIFT TODAY...

I HAVEN'T...
...TOLD HIM YET...
I MEAN, EVEN I'VE—
BUT... I THINK HE CAN TELL SOME-THING'S WRONG...

RIGHT.
SINCE YOU'RE TWINS.
YOU COULD ALWAYS TELL WHAT THE OTHER WAS FEELING SINCE WE WERE KIDS.

WHY DID YOU KILL?

NAI-CHAN, THAT WAS TOO DIRECT ...!
?
WELL ...

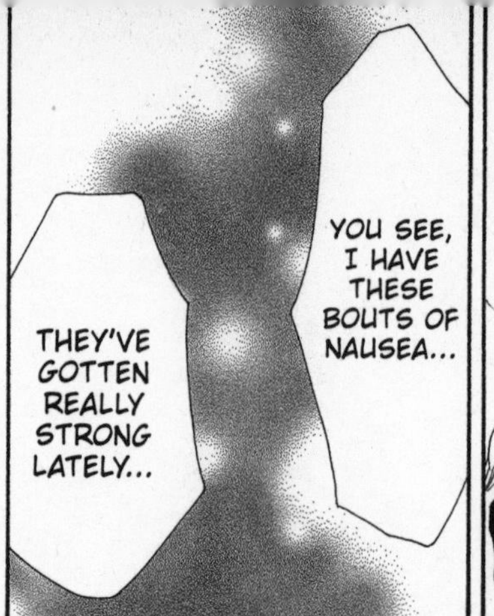
YOU SEE, I HAVE THESE BOUTS OF NAUSEA...
THEY'VE GOTTEN REALLY STRONG LATELY...

THEY WOULD MAKE ME ZONE OUT...
...AND WHEN I'D COME BACK TO MY SENSES, I WOULD FIND BLOOD ON MY CLOTHES...
I COULD NEVER REMEMBER WHAT HAD HAPPENED ...
BUT THEN...

...RECENTLY, SOMETHING CHANGED...
WHEN I CAME TO...

...THERE WERE...
...ALL THESE DEAD PEOPLE AROUND ME.
BAN (SLAM)
AAAAUGH!!?
BAS-TARDS ...

WHAT ARE YOU DOING TO TSUBAME!?
DOGA (FWOOM)
WHAAA!?
YOTAKA!!!
...
STOP! YOU'RE MISTAKEN!
IT'S GAREKI!
... GAREKI?
WHAT?
YOU'RE STILL ALIVE?

RII (KREE)
RII
ARE YOU...
...SURE ABOUT THIS?
GAN (CLANG)
HUH?
THERE ARE TWO BEDS HERE. I'D SAY WE LUCKED OUT.
THE THREE OF US SQUEEZ-ING ONTO ONE BED WOULD'VE BEEN PRETTY UNCOM-FORTABLE.
BUT...JUST BARGING INTO A STRANGER'S HOUSE AND USING THEIR BEDS...?
YOU HEARD TSUBAME, DIDN'T YOU?
THE PEOPLE ACROSS FROM THEM JUST UP AND LEFT IN THE MIDDLE OF THE NIGHT. SO SINCE THEIR HOUSE IS ABANDONED...
...IT'S TOTALLY FINE TO STAY HERE!
THAT'S THE PART THAT MAKES ME WONDER IF WE SHOULD...
HEY, GAREKI-KUN?
WHAT'S YOUR RELATION TO THE TWINS?

HUH?
DO YOU MIND MY ASK-ING?
NOT REALLY, I GUESS.

LET'S SEE...
I MUST'VE BEEN AROUND EIGHT YEARS OLD WHEN MY PARENTS SOLD ME.
HUH!?
WAIT, WAS IT REALLY OKAY TO ASK, THEN ...!?

OR AT LEAST...
...I CONSIDERED THEM MY PARENTS.
ANY-WAY...

...THINGS WENT PRETTY BADLY FOR ME IN THE SHIP THAT I WAS PACKED OFF IN.

ALL OF US WHO'D BEEN SOLD...
...WERE STUFFED INTO ONE ROOM TOGETHER.
ONCE THAT HAPPENED, IT STARTED, OF COURSE.
THE BULLYING OF THE WEAK. WHAT COMPLETE BULLSHIT.
I WASN'T ACTUALLY ALL THAT WEAK.
BUT I WAS THE SMALLEST OF THE LOT, SO THAT'S WHAT THEY TOOK ME FOR. THEY TIED ME UP...
...AND KEPT ME FROM THE TWO MEALS A DAY THAT WERE SO THOUGHTFULLY PROVIDED FOR US.
BUT...
...THAT WAS WHEN I STARTED REALIZING...
...THERE WAS SOMETHING IN THE FOOD.
THE OTHERS WERE GETTING WEAKER BY THE DAY.

ONE NIGHT, THE SHIP RAN AGROUND WHEN WE HIT SOME STORMY SEAS ...
...AND I TOOK MY CHANCE TO ESCAPE.
IT WAS SHEER LUCK THAT I EVEN MADE IT TO SHORE ALIVE.
I PICKED A DIRECTION THAT SEEMED LIKELY TO LEAD TO FOOD...
...AND JUST STARTED WALKING.
BUT I GOT TO A POINT WHERE I WAS SO EXHAUSTED I THOUGHT I'D NEVER MOVE AGAIN.

THAT WAS WHEN TSUBAKI FOUND ME.

SHE SAVED MY LIFE.
TSUBAME AND YOTAKA WERE HER LITTLE SISTER AND BROTHER.

TSUBAKI ...
...WAS BETRAYED—MURDERED—BY THE MAN SHE LOVED.

I DON'T KNOW THE FACE OF THE MAN WHO KILLED HER...
...BUT IF I EVER FIND HIM, I WILL KILL HIM.

HUH?
SHALL I GIVE YOU A HUG?
WHAT ... ...THE ...?
ぶるぶる
BURU (QUIVER) BURU
ぶるぶる
BURU BURU

IT'S SAID THAT THE LOVE IN A HUG CAN HEAL THE HEART OF A MISTREATED CHILD—
YOU'RE THE CHILD HERE!!
くわっしゃー
KUWASSHAA (SNARL)
KILLING IS BAD. IT WAS HARD TO UNDERSTAND EVERYTHING, BUT, GAREKI, I DON'T WANT YOU TO KILL!

BOTH OF YOU...
...JUST SHUT UP...!!
RII (KREE)
RII

I...
...DID TOO.
IT'S FINE.
IF TSUBAME REALLY IS A VARUGA NOW...
HOW DID IT HAPPEN?
AND WHEN?
NO...
I ALWAYS SUSPECTED SOMETHING WAS UP WITH THAT MEDICINE...
THEN, COULD THE MAN WHO USED AND KILLED TSUBAKI...
...BE CONNECTED TO THE ORGANIZATION THAT CIRCUS IS AFTER?
HEY...

CAN PEOPLE WHO'VE TURNED INTO VARUGA ...
...EVER TURN BACK?
...!
I SEE.
GA (SNAG)
!?
A BODY!?
... THERE'S ...
...SOME-THING DRAWN ON HIM.

THEY AREN'T DRAWINGS.
THEY'RE CUTS...
BUT...
...I'VE SEEN THAT PATTERN BEFORE...
BACK THEN...
...I DIDN'T THINK ANYTHING OF THE SHAPE OF HER WOUNDS.
BUT THOSE PATTERNS WERE ON TSUBAKI'S DEAD BODY TOO.
THE SAME SCARS AS HER ...
WHICH MEANS ...
...IT'S THE SAME KILLER...
THEN...
DOKU (BADMP)
ドク…
"I DON'T KNOW THE FACE OF THE MAN WHO KILLED HER...
"...BUT IF I EVER FIND HIM..."
YURA (STAGGER)
ユラ…
POTA (DRIP)
ポタ…

To be continued in KARNEVAL 2!

KARNEVAL

Bonus Comic 1 - Who's the Child Here?

OH, HON-ESTLY! IT MUST HAVE BEEN EVA-NEE-SAN!
WHO ELSE WOULD STICK SOMETHING LIKE THIS ON MY BACK?
WHAT'S "LITTLE KID" SUPPOSED TO MEAN ANYWAY!?
IT WAS ONLY BECAUSE THE SHEEP WERE STARING SO HARD AT ME...
...THAT I EVEN NOTICED IT AT ALL.
I NEED TO FIND HER AND COMPLAIN.
HUH?
?
WHAT?
LITTLE KID
JII (STARE)
JII
ARE YOU STILL EATING!?
...
HEY! PUT IT ALL IN YOUR MOUTH, AND DON'T YOU WASTE ANY OF IT!
AWA (PANIC)
MOGU (MUNCH)
NAI-CHAN! GAREKI-K...
EH—
WAIT A— GAREKI-KUN!
ON YOUR BACK!
ON YOUR BACK!
HUH?
NIYA (GRIN)
NIYA
NEE-SAN!
MOGU
MOGU
PET-SITTER

THE HOLE THAT NAI FELL THROUGH LAST TIME...
...IS PART OF THE SHEEP'S NETWORK OF MAIN-TENANCE TUNNELS.
LISTENING...

どきどき
DOKI (BADUM) DOKI
SOO (SIFF)
BIKU (TWITCH)
びくびく
BIKU
カタン
KATAN (KLANG)

NYU (POPP)
!

UCHU (SHMOOCH)
...
...?
A FIRST KISS?

Bonus Comic 3 - Inherited Traits

DR. AKARI ... COULD YOU PLEASE TAKE A LOOK AT THIS?
YOU AND THE TEAM SHOULD BE ABLE TO DO FOLLOW-UP ON THAT ADJUSTMENT YOURSELVES.
BUT, SIR... WE CAN UNDERSTAND YOUR DATA, BUT...
IF YOU'RE SO INCOMPETENT THAT YOU CAN'T HANDLE A PROBLEM OF THIS LEVEL, THE ONLY CAREER HIGH YOU SHOULD BE AIMING FOR IS BECOMING A HUMAN GUINEA PIG.

WHAAAT?
DOCTOR, WAIT!
HMPH!
HOW IN THE WORLD DID AKARI TURN OUT THIS WAY DESPITE HAVING HAD ME AS HIS MENTOR?
HE'S A HOPE-LESS CASE...
DOC-TOR!

SINCE YOU RARELY RETURN TO THE RESEARCH TOWER...
...THERE ARE STACKS OF DOCUMENTS AWAITING YOUR APPROVAL!
PLEASE, YOU MUST LOOK AT THEM TODAY—
WHAAAT?
I DON'T WANT TO! YOU'RE ALL SUCH BRIGHT PEOPLE, I'M SURE YOU CAN TAKE CARE OF IT IN A FLASH YOURSELVES! I'D LIKE YOU TO HANDLE IT FOR ME!

...
I THINK YOU'RE ACTUALLY QUITE SIMILAR.
AT THE CORE...

IF YOU'D LIKE TO UNDER-GO MY HEALING TREAT-MENT, JOIN US AGAIN NEXT TIME!

—AKARI

Pre-serialization
One-Shot
GUUU (GRUMBLE)
JIII (STARE)
NAI?
GAREKI, THAT LOOKS YUMMY.
EH?
WHOA...
SUPER-HIGH-GRADE FOOD...
THERE'S A TON TOO... SOMEONE'S GOT A LOT OF MONEY!
NO CAN DO.
I CAN'T AFFORD IT.
OKAY.
VERY OBEDIENT...
......

PETA (SET)
GAREKI?
WHAT ARE YOU DOING?
WHY SHOULD THE GREAT KIICHI HAVE TO GO ON A SHOPPING RUN!?
AND WITH A MAN FROM TEAM 2, OF ALL THINGS!
SO YOU SAY, BUT REALLY... YOU BOUGHT SO MANY EXPENSIVE THINGS...
THIS IS GOVERNMENT MONEY, YOU KNOW.
PI (BEEP)
HERE YOU GO, CAR!
TIME TO HEAD OUT.
BUUN (VROOO)
BURORORO (VRRRM)
GAGON (CLONK)
HUH!?
EEEK!?
ZUGAN (BOING)
DON (WHAM)
IT FLIPPED ON ITS SIDE.
EEEK!
WHAT ARE YOU DOING!? THIS IS WHY I HATE TEAM 2!!
YOU KEEP COMPLAINING ABOUT TEAM 2 AS THOUGH TEAM 1'S SO MUCH BETTER THAN US!
WE ARE BETTER!!
BARA (SPILL)
BARA

OH NO.
HOW TERRIBLE. WE SHOULD HELP THEM.
INSTI-GATOR
NAI.
HELP THEM PICK UP THEIR STUFF.
AND ASK IF THEY'RE OKAY.
OZU (TIMIDLY)
UM...
UH...
MUGIGI (STREEETCH)
ARE YOU OKAY?
EH?
UH...
KYUUN (TWINGE)
THANK YOU! SORRY FOR THIS MESS!
HMPH!
YOU'RE SUCH A NICE KID. AND SO CUTE! SO DIFFERENT FROM MY COMPANION HERE...
GAN (THONK)
PAKA (CRACK)
AWW...
UM, THIS ONE SEEMS TO HAVE CRACKED OPEN.
I'LL BUY IT AT A DISCOUNT, IF YOU'RE GAME?
IRA (IRK)
IRA
UGH, YOU CAN TAKE IT IF YOU WANT!!
YOU CAN'T PROFIT OFF BROKEN THINGS ANYHOW.

Special One-Shot • End

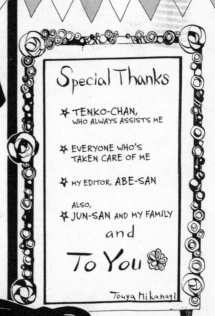

HELLO, EVERYONE! THIS IS TOUYA. THANK YOU VERY MUCH FOR READING *KARNEVAL* VOLUME 2. I REALLY HOPE YOU ENJOYED SEEING MORE OF THE WORLD OF *KARNEVAL* WITH NAI AND FRIENDS. FOR THIS VOLUME, IN ADDITION TO THE BONUS COMICS, I WAS ABLE TO INCLUDE A SPECIAL ONE-SHOT COMIC THAT I DREW BEFORE THE SERIES BEGAN SERIALIZATION. ANYTIME I LOOK BACK AT MY OLD WORK, THOUGH, I ALWAYS FEEL SO EMBARRASSED. YOGI'S HAIR IS SO SHORT! TO GET TO THE LENGTH IT IS IN THE MAIN STORY, IT MUST'VE BEEN AT LEAST SIX MONTHS' GROWTH AFTER THIS STORY...I GUESS? OR MAYBE HE JUST GREW A LOT AS A PERSON BETWEEN THEN AND NOW. HE DOES SEEM MORE MATURE IN THE MAIN STORY, DOESN'T HE?

MY EDITOR HADN'T SEEN THIS STORY IN A LONG TIME EITHER AND EXCLAIMED, "YOGI LOOKS SO YOUNG!!" UPON SEEING IT AGAIN. BUT I'VE ACTUALLY BEEN THINKING, MAYBE I SHOULD START PUTTING CHARACTER PROFILES FOR NAI AND GAREKI AND EVERYONE IN THESE BONUS AREAS. I DO ALSO HAVE ADDITIONAL INFO ON THE WORLD OF *KARNEVAL* ON MY BLOG, SO EVEN THOUGH I DON'T UPDATE IT THAT FREQUENTLY, PLEASE DO COME CHECK IT OUT SOMETIME.

—TOUYA

SEE YOU SOON!

Special Thanks
TENKO-CHAN, WHO ALWAYS ASSISTS ME
EVERYONE WHO'S TAKEN CARE OF ME
MY EDITOR, ABE-SAN
ALSO, JUN-SAN AND MY FAMILY
and
To You
Touya Mikanagi

Japanese Volume 4
Under Jacket Bonus Comic
GREETINGS, LADIES ALL ACROSS THE NATION! ♥
I'D LOVE TO CAPTURE YOU JUST LIKE THIS.
IN MY ARMS... ☆

BUT HIRATO-SAN TOLD ME TO GREET THE READERS!

THAT HURTS, TSUKUMO-CHAAAN~!

HIRATO!? SO IT WAS HIRATO, HUH!?

HEY, GAREKI? WHAT'S THIS BOX?

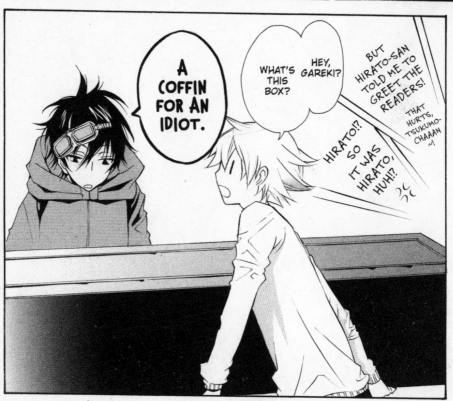

A COFFIN FOR AN IDIOT.

Japanese Volume 2
Under Jacket Bonus Comic
AS I CANNOT HEAR YOUR ADORABLE VOICE...
...WON'T YOU PUT YOUR SWEET LIPS AGAINST MY EAR AND WHISPER YOUR WORDS TO ME?
WELL, MY LADY?

カッ
KA (FLASH)

KRONE SAPHIR!

ドーン
DOOON (BOOM)

もく
MOKU (PUFF)

もく
MOKU

?

I HAVE TO SEE TO AN UNSEEMLY BIT OF BUSI-NESS.

SO DON'T COME IN HERE FOR A BIT, ALL RIIIGHT?

?

GO ON AND PLAY OVER THERE, OKAY?

I MUST DEFEND ALL THE WOMEN OF THE WORLD...

KARNEVAL

Read on for a preview of
the next volume!

Score 13:
Flightless Wings

YOTAKA ...!
YOU ...
くちゅ
KUCHA (MUNCH)
PICH (SLURP)
ちゅぱっ
CHUPA (SMUCK)
I'M...
GA—
...HUN-GRY.

LISTEN UP, NAI.

YOUR GOAL'S TO SEE KAROKU AGAIN, RIGHT?

......
I DON'T LIKE SAYING LAME STUFF LIKE THIS, BUT...

THEN, YOU NEED TO KEEP A COOL HEAD AND STAY OUT OF UNNECESSARY STUFF.
USE CIRCUS, AND FIND YOUR WAY FORWARD!

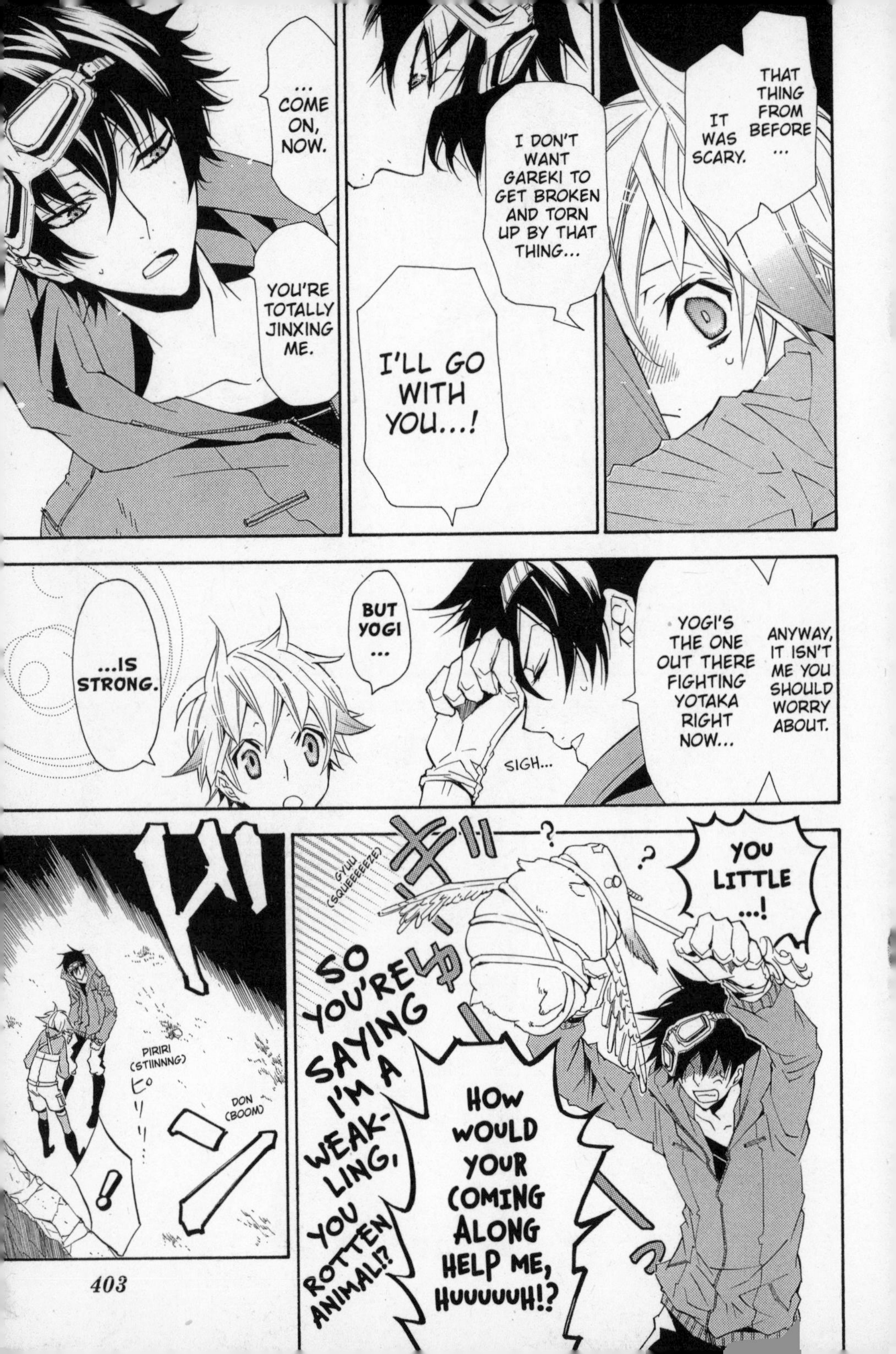

THAT THING FROM BEFORE ...

IT WAS SCARY.

I DON'T WANT GAREKI TO GET BROKEN AND TORN UP BY THAT THING...

I'LL GO WITH YOU...!

... COME ON, NOW.

YOU'RE TOTALLY JINXING ME.

ANYWAY, IT ISN'T ME YOU SHOULD WORRY ABOUT.
YOGI'S THE ONE OUT THERE FIGHTING YOTAKA RIGHT NOW...
SIGH...
BUT YOGI ...
...IS STRONG.

YOU LITTLE ...!
GYUU (SQUEEEEEEZE)
SO YOU'RE SAYING I'M A WEAKLING, YOU ROTTEN ANIMAL!?
HOW WOULD YOUR COMING ALONG HELP ME, HUUUUUH!?
PIRIRI (STIINNNG)
DON (BOOM)

THAT'S THE ROAD WE TOOK HERE.

IF YOU GO STRAIGHT DOWN IT, YOU'LL GET BACK TO KARASUNA. GOT IT?

GAREKI ...

I'LL LEND YOU MY JACKET, SO JUST KEEP THE HOOD UP AND TRY NOT TO DRAW ANY ATTENTION—

NO!

WHOA!

HEY ...

NO!

NO ...

GU (SQUEEZE)

NO!

WHAT'S WRONG?

THERE HE IS!
THERE'S GAREKI!
...DID YOU NEED SOMETHING?
UM, "NEED SOMETHING?" UM, WELL...
...
WE WERE JUST WONDERING WHERE YOU'D GONE OFF TO, AND...WE JUST, UM...
WE JUST NOTICED WE HADN'T SEEN YOU FOR A WHILE, SO...
...NAI.
YOU HEAD BACK ON YOUR OWN FROM HERE.

"DO AS I SAY," HE SAYS. SCREW THAT!
LIKE I WOULD.

'COS THOSE PEOPLE ARE...

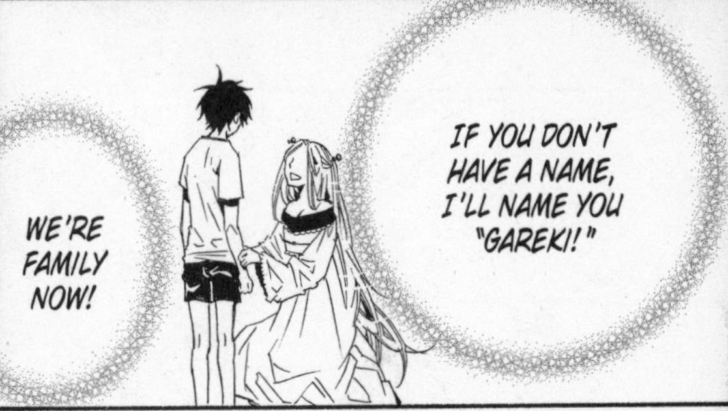
IF YOU DON'T HAVE A NAME, I'LL NAME YOU "GAREKI!"
WE'RE FAMILY NOW!

HOW DUMB. WHAT DOES THAT MATTER?

COME ON!
WE CAN'T START DINNER UNTIL YOU COME TO THE TABLE.
GUU (GRUMBLE)
HUH!
HUH?
YOU MEAN DINNER'S A THING THAT YOU EAT TOGETHER?

WHAT'S THAT CONFUSED LOOK FOR?
I BROUGHT THESE SCRAPS BACK FROM THE FACTORY FOR YA TO PLAY WITH.
YOU'RE ALWAYS FIDDLIN' WITH THINGS, AIN'T YA?

WE'LL MEET BACK UP IN KARASUNA, OKAY?
SORRY I CAN'T ACCOMPANY YOU...
I'LL SEE YOU AGAIN LATER.
BYU (FWOOSH)
...!
YOGI.
...SHIT!
NAI! COME ON!!
GUN (TUG)

DAN (THUMP)
GAREKI-KUN.
TAKE NAI-CHAN, AND LEAVE THIS VILLAGE RIGHT NOW!
WHA ...!?
LIKE HELL!! I NEED TO TALK TO YOTAKA...!
THERE'S NO WAY TO TALK TO HIM ANYMORE.
DO AS I SAY FOR ONCE BEFORE YOU GET YOURSELF KILLED.
HERE HE COMES!
FU (VOOSH)

DOGO
(BOOM)